I Can Manage

I Can Manage

A Practical Approach to School Foodservice Management

Jay Caton & Mary Nix

A CBI Book
Published by Van Nostrand Reinhold Company
—*New York*

A CBI Book
(CBI is an imprint of Van Nostrand Reinhold Company Inc.)
Copyright © 1986 by Van Nostrand Reinhold Company Inc.

Library of Congress Catalog Card Number 85-27135

ISBN 0-442-21766-8

All rights reserved. No part of this work covered by the copyright hereon may be reproduced or used in any form or by any means—graphic, electronic, or mechanical, including photocopying, recording, taping, or information storage and retrieval systems—without written permission of the publisher.

Printed in the United States of America

Designed by Kathryn Parise

Van Nostrand Reinhold Company Inc.
115 Fifth Avenue
New York, New York 10003

Van Nostrand Reinhold Company Limited
Molly Millars Lane
Wokingham, Berkshire RG11 2PY, England

Van Nostrand Reinhold
480 La Trobe Street
Melbourne, Victoria 3000, Australia

Macmillan of Canada
Division of Canada Publishing Corporation
164 Commander Boulevard
Agincourt, Ontario M1S 3C7, Canada

16 15 14 13 12 11 10 9 8 7 6 5 4 3 2 1

Library of Congress Cataloging-in-Publication Data

Caton, Jay.
  I can manage.

  "A CBI book."
  Includes index.
  1. Food service management. 2. School lunchrooms, cafeterias, etc. I. Nix, Mary. II. Title.
TX911.3.M27C38   1986   642'.5'068   85-27135
ISBN 0-442-21766-8

Contents

Preface   vii

An Introduction to Miss Jessie   1

Your Management Image Is Showing   9

Jessie, I Need Help   33

Where Are You Coming From?   37

My Time Is Your Time   53

Have You Got a Minute?   58

Edie   66

The Right Equation   71

The Casserole Caper (Part 1)   89

What's for Lunch?   94

The Casserole Caper (Part 2)   107

Managing Nagging Problems   112

The Last Day   123

Index   129

We never met Miss Jessie, but we know someone who did: Louise Sublette. Louise was a consultant with the Tennessee Department of Education. For many years she traveled the state, working with school foodservice managers. She liked the work. She loved the people.

Years later, when she became a national leader in the foodservice profession, Louise focused her efforts on helping school managers gain the recognition that they deserved. And the way she did it was to talk about Miss Jessie, a pioneer school foodservice manager in Tennessee.

Louise had a way with a story. She would start off slowly and build it with remarks that had you laughing until tears came to your eyes. And just about the time you saw the punch line coming, she would throw you a curve and you would end up with a moral that had the truth of the ages in it.

Neither one of us has either the sense of humor or the wisdom of Louise Sublette. But our memories of her are intertwined with her stories about Miss Jessie. It is to Louise and all the thousands of Miss Jessies who perform so capably in this nation's foodservice profession that this book is dedicated.

Preface

Every school day, 24 million customers pass through the serving lines of the fourth largest foodservice operation in America. They are offered meals that meet strict nutritional standards, that are inexpensive, and, most important, that taste good.

It takes time and talent to turn flour and butter, vegetables and fruit, meat and eggs into meals that customers like to eat. Above all, it takes good management, composed of equal parts of common sense, honesty, pride, "people skills," public relations, ability to handle stress, a love of children, financial savvy, an easy-to-get-to sense of humor, and continuing education.

That is all it takes!

And that is why school foodservice is one of the most successful, economically sound programs in the nation. As good as it is, it can become better. The people who can make that happen are the managers of local school programs. The buck starts and stops with them and the people who assist them in food preparation and service.

School foodservice over the past few years has undergone enormous changes. Dependent as it is upon federal dollars for meal reimbursements, the program suffered financial shock as a result of funding cuts in 1981. More than 2,500 programs left the National School Lunch Program in the year that followed. Some of those schools discontinued their foodservice programs. Others modified their operations to avoid having to provide a full meal pattern. Still others turned to management companies to provide students with foodservice. Food management companies contract with local Boards of Education and supply food on a for-profit basis. By 1984, about 7 percent of all school foodservice operations were run by food management companies.

The vast majority of school foodservice professionals, however, dealt with the funding cuts themselves. They dealt with them in many cases by raising meal prices. When they did that, they lost customers, as many as 1 percent of their customers for every penny of increase in the meal price.

But the people who prepare food in schools are tough nuts to crack. Most met the challenge with the three M's—merchandising, menus, and management. Our Miss Jessie stories are meant to illustrate the importance of one good person in a school foodservice operation.

Partly as a result of the funding cuts, partly in answer to the explosion of fast-food operations, and partly because they are sound businesspersons, school foodservice people redoubled their marketing efforts to merchandise their food more attractively. They created new promotions and contests. They recognized anew that students and faculties are customers and encouraged their participation.

Better food merchandising was one way to reach customers. New menu items were another. After examining how customers were spending their food dollars away from their classrooms, school foodservice staffs intensified their offerings of popular ethnic foods. They increasingly offered food choices rather than filling plates with food that might or might not be eaten. They introduced salad, potato, Mexican food bars. They offered individual items. They served popular foods more often.

They coped—and they survived. They survived because of better merchandising and more menu choices. But perhaps the real key to the continuation of the programs in so many schools was improved management of foodservice operations. Directors looked at their district-level programs and reevaluated the ways they let out bids and purchased food. They looked at labor use and found ways to increase the efficiency of the people who prepared meals. They realized anew the importance of updating the skills needed by those preparing and serving food. And administrators are now recognizing and rewarding foodservice staffs for that training.

But most of all, school administrators appreciated all over again the importance of school foodservice managers. As long as schools have had nutrition programs, managers and their assistants ultimately have determined the quality of food offered to customers and thus affected whether bottom lines have been written in red or black ink.

School foodservice has experienced its financial crunches. It will again. And it will survive as long as the competent people who operate local school programs remember their commitment to customers, make the best possible use of their resources, and continue to sharpen their management skills.

This book was written to help them do just that.

An Introduction to Miss Jessie

Miss Jessie was the oldest of three Logan children. The Logans were as poor as church mice, but they shared pride and hope and love as they scratched away on the small farm that was never quite paid for.

Jessie was the one the family depended on for its meals, its sewing, its clean clothes. The meals were plain. The clothes were washed in a tub on a board that had suffered through three generations. The Logans depended on Jessie because her mother, Carrie, had never quite recovered from little Jamie's birth. Jessie, who was only fourteen when Carrie passed away, was a pretty girl—no raving beauty, to be sure, but with her dark hair, wide brown eyes, and ample figure, she was worth a second glance. Some young men around Middleville thought so too. There was one in particular. His name was Tom Pritchard.

Jessie was well aware of Tom too, but she had other things on her mind that were more important: raising a brother and a sister and making sure that her father ate on time. That last chore was not so easy, because her father seemed to be more interested in drinking on time. Pug Logan did a lot of drinking. He used a mason jar that he refilled often from Jeb Edwards's still, which was down the road a piece and up in the trees.

When he drank hard, Pug became a different person. Normally, he was a gentle, hard-working man who cared for his family. During Jessie's growing-up years, Pug didn't drink too much. But there were some binges once in a while, and when Pug turned nasty, the kids and Carrie felt the back of his hand a lot.

When Carrie died, something in Pug died too. His mason jar became his constant companion. Jessie and the other kids stayed out of his way. When he wanted company, he'd go down the road to Jeb's and sit around the still and jaw.

At Jeb's one Saturday night in late October, Pug turned nasty over something that no one remembers. People said it was an accident. Nobody knew for sure. Voices got louder, fingers punched chests in anger, and Pug was killed.

Jessie and the kids buried him next to Carrie. Jessie was sixteen. After the funeral, eight of the Logan kids' aunts and uncles pulled Jessie aside and announced their plans for the "poor orphans." Hettie would take Jamie; Ed and Martha would take Hester. But that was as far as they got. Jessie minced no words. The family would stay together. Period. They would manage, she was sure of that. Jessie sewed well, and she would take in sewing from Middleville. Jessie made her point. Before the family split them up, they would have had to put Jessie in the ground next to Pug and Carrie.

If life was hard *with* Pug, it was worse for Jessie and the kids after they buried him. The bowls of food at suppertime were fewer, and there was less food in them.

Two years after Pug died, Tom Pritchard came courting. And three months later, Jessie became Mrs. Tom Pritchard. Tom had a good job in Middleville at the lumberyard. He made extra money roofing and painting houses. He worked fast and well, and Middleville always had more work for him than he could do.

Hester and Jamie finished high school. Soon after that, Hester got married and moved to Middleville. Jamie joined the navy. He liked to travel. They heard from him once in a while.

Tom and Jessie had three babies, and, as with most families in the late 1940s, there was never quite enough money to go around. Jessie had to help out. Though she still took in sewing, Jessie was always the one that the town turned to when a banquet was needed. She *did* know how to cook what people liked to eat. When Jessie did a banquet, the guests always raved about the food.

For nine years Tom and Jessie savored and deepened their love for their family and each other.

One muggy, late-June morning, Jessie was in the backyard hanging her family's damp, sweet-smelling clothes on the line. She was humming and thinking about what she'd have for dinner. What would Tom like, she wondered.

She didn't hear the car stop in front of the house or the footsteps behind her. "Jessie." The voice was low. Startled, she turned, smiling, to see Bill Jenkins. Bill was Tom's boss at the lumberyard. The look on Bill's face erased Jessie's smile. The blood drained from her face.

"I've got some bad news, Jessie."

Her words came out as a moan. "Oh, dear God, no!"

" 'Fraid so, Jessie. He just pitched forward and fell off the big Evans house." Bill reached out and pulled her into his arms. And she cried.

Tom didn't leave much insurance. There was enough to bury him properly and to pay off the mortgage, but Jessie knew that she'd have to go to work. Jessie was alone and yet not alone. Middleville knew Jessie, and its people cared about her. And they had a need.

The days of the one-room schools, the ones that Jessie and her children and Jessie's parents had gone to, were numbered. For a lot of good reasons, consolidated schools were the future and Middleville's was due to open in the fall. Because students were coming in from the country and because the school was being built out on the edge of town, kids were going to need to eat their lunch at school. Middleville Consolidated had a cafeteria and a kitchen; what it didn't have was a cook.

The school board chairman was Bill Jenkins, Tom's former boss, and he offered some advice to the new superintendent. He told him that Jessie Pritchard was a smart woman, she cooked well, and she needed a job.

Jessie was surprised when she got the phone call, but she agreed to go into town and talk with the superintendent. After they had talked for a while about Middleville Consolidated and kids and cooking, Jessie was offered a job. "Will you run our lunchroom, Mrs. Pritchard?"

Jessie wanted the job, but she let the superintendent know that she didn't know the first thing about preparing a meal every day for 200 people.

The superintendent smiled and answered, "Who around Middleville does?"

And Jessie smiled back. He was right. She could do the job as well as anyone else—and maybe better. So Jessie went to work.

Frazzled was the only word to describe the way Jessie felt that November day of Middleville Consolidated's first year.

She had started to work the morning after Labor Day with a yeasty mixture of concern, excitement, and determination. Now, after two months, all three feelings had gone very flat.

Jessie's earlier concern about whether she could have a meal ready every day for 200 kids wasn't gone altogether. But as long as she had a storeroom, a can opener, and five hands, she could manage.

And that first excitement? It was well under control. She had looked forward to serving kids their noon meal, but somehow all she had seen for two months were hands scooting trays and the tops of tousled heads. There didn't seem to be either the time or the chance to do anything more than make sure that full plates were thrust into outstretched hands. Hands connected to faceless bodies.

That original determination? It was still there, but it was in another form now. Jessie was determined in those days just to have a good meal ready every day at 11:20. What it cost to put that meal on the line concerned her, but not overly so—that is, until the end of September, when she had to fill out some strange forms. She got a shock when she finished them. Even figuring in the nickel a meal that Middleville Consolidated would get back for every meal that she had served that month, she spent more than she had taken in. Jessie made a decision right then to continue to prepare a good meal each day, but she was also determined that she would do it within her budget. In October she had come close.

But that particular November day had been a disaster right from the start. Jessie began to suspect that it was going to be one of those days when her alarm clock didn't let out a peep. Fortunately, one of her kids did. Then, after getting them off to school, she had trouble getting the car engine to turn over. That was the best the day got.

The macaroni boiled over. The gallon of milk that she'd planned to use had soured. The opener had a fight with a can of peas—and the peas won. The rolls came out of the oven looking like rows of soiled toadstools. Jessie was convinced that if it hadn't been for the brown Betty, not much could have saved the meal from being condemned by all but the starving of China.

After the last student from the last class had been served, Jessie slumped into the chair by the cash box recently vacated by Rita, the school secretary and a long-time friend.

Jessie didn't see young Billy Wilden when he came back into the serving area. She started when the small voice asked, "Miss Jessie, could I have a straw, please?"

Jessie took her hand from her forehead and looked up into the eyes of the sober-faced fifth-grader. She smiled at him. Tentatively, Billy smiled back.

"Why, sure. . . . Now, let me see. You're . . ."

"I'm Billy Wilden, Miss Jessie."

"Well, Billy," Jessie said, getting up and walking behind the counter, "let's see about getting you a straw."

As she handed the straw across the counter, Billy said, "Thank you, Miss Jessie." Turning to go with his head lowered, he stopped and turned halfway around.

"Miss Jessie," Billy said.

"Yes, Billy?"

"Miss Jessie, you make the best brown apples in the world. Even better than Grandma's." Quickly, he turned and left, his face already beginning to redden.

Jessie stared at the spot where Billy had been. Her mouth formed the words, but at that moment they were far more than words. They were an acknowledgment of a gratitude that would last for a very long time.

"Thank you, Billy."

The alarm clock that didn't go off, the mess on the stove, the rolls that were an embarrassment, the dirty dishes waiting to be washed—at that moment they all suddenly seemed like puny annoyances. Billy Wilden liked her cooking, and if Billy liked it, some other kids might like it too.

The stove was cleaned and the dishes were washed. In the length of time that that took, Miss Jessie (that was what she was called from then on) came to some conclusions that would grow and deepen to become convictions as the years passed.

Her students were not just a lot of hands and downturned heads, but individuals to be treated as customers who were friends and who deserved the best that she could give. The image that she—and later her assistants—projected across that serving line was reflected in the faces and attitudes of those who passed through that line. Whether it was "brown apples" or pizza or chicken gravy, Miss Jessie planned her menus around what her kids liked to eat. She gave her customers what they wanted, and her customers came back the next day.

On that tenth day of November, with a rotten day behind her and a dirty kitchen around her, Miss Jessie came home with a profession to which she would give a number of years—and gain a lifetime.

And Billy Wilden's son, young Tom, was partial to Miss Jessie's "brown apples" too.

Did you ever notice that just about the time you are getting a little bit ahead with your budget, the dish machine begins making strange and wonderful noises?

Did you ever notice that, if you followed some recipes to the letter, you would end up with something that had all the appeal of pickled eel?

Your Management Image Is Showing

"To eat or not to eat" is a school lunch dilemma that parents and students consider daily. The image of the staff and program can be the determining factor. If the program is to be successful, employees must be customer-conscious. Images cannot be bought or sold. They have to be earned. Once a bad image is established, people cling to that impression of an individual or program, regardless of what is done later. Bad images can be formed with just one incident, and they are hard to live down.

Changing a bad image requires a great deal of work. You must show *consistently* that you have changed. Once you have succeeded in improving your image, be very careful. One slip can put you right back where you started.

Customers have an image or mental picture of the manager and of the staff that is guided by attitude and enthusiasm, appearance, and skills.

The image that customers have of the program is influenced by staff, speed and efficiency of service, relationships and interaction among customers and community, quantity and quality of food served, appearance of the food, and cleanliness and appearance of the facility.

We will examine these images and at the same time do some self-evaluation.

Managing Image with Enthusiasm and a Positive Attitude

The attitude of the staff has a greater impact on the image of the program than any other single factor. Whether or not students buy meals and whether they eat meals after they buy them are often determined by the attitude of the staff who serves them.

The food can be great, with many choices to meet the taste preference of each customer, but if the staff on the serving line has a case of "negative-itis," little else matters. The employees who have the best attitude and best coordination should be assigned to the serving line and the dish-return window. If an employee is having a bad day with a good case of negative-itis, assign him or her to the clean end of the dish machine. He or she will contaminate fewer people there.

The cashier interacts personally with each student who comes through the line. In addition to being accurate, she must have a positive, enthusiastic attitude in order to present a good image of the program and make the customers happy that they bought a school meal.

Positive attitudes and enthusiasm cannot be bought or mandated, but they are infectious. Both will make people happy to be around you. Both will help to create a great image.

But now about that negative-itis that sometimes can affect even the best of managers and assistants. The accompanying chart suggests some of the problems as well as some ways to look for solutions.

When students enter a serving line, several of their senses are going at once. Their sense of smell can be turned on by aromas that start the juices flowing. Their sense of sight can be turned on by how you present the food you have prepared. Another sense is more subtle. Their personal radar will tell them in an instant if they are truly welcome as customers in your cafeteria. The minute that you take them for granted is the minute that your image changes for the worse.

> ***Did you ever notice that if the first student through the line grumbles about the food, the last one knows about it before the first one has reached the cashier?***

Are You Suffering From Negative-itis?

Symptoms of Negative-itis	*Cure Questions*
You see school foodservice as an impossible chore with no future	What have you *done* to strengthen the future?
You think the kids you serve are troublemakers who cannot be pleased	Have you tried to "tune in" on students' food and meal preferences without being defensive?
You criticize students for failing to enjoy your great menus	Are these menus that *you* would enjoy? (Remember your customers are a new generation.)
You believe that the success of a meal is judged by the ease of preparation	Have you looked in the garbage can lately? Do you know what your food and labor costs are?
You snap, "You do not know what we go through just to get this meal prepared!"	Are you budgeting your time and using it wisely?
You see your co-workers or superiors as "power hounds"	Why are you so insecure?
You believe that others are gossiping about you or trying to "do you in"	Are you guilty? What have you done to make others feel good about working with you?
You feel depressed and "put upon" when the faculty or principal makes suggestions	Do you consider yourself a part of the team?
You excuse poor cooperation by saying, "My folks are not interested. They won't go to meetings. They won't join our professional association, either"	What kind of salesman are you? Do *you* think it is important to grow professionally?
You believe that the dining room is just a place for the students to eat	Is the atmosphere in the dining room inviting? What kind of personality does it show?

12 ◊ *I Can Manage*

To examine your own situation, take the following Customer Test.

Customer Test

Do You Turn Customers Away?			Do You Invite Customers to Enjoy School Meals?		
Yes	No		Yes	No	
☐	☐	Do you always frown and never smile?	☐	☐	Do you smile and show interest in school activities?
☐	☐	Do you make snide, curt, or uncomplimentary remarks to students or about students?	☐	☐	Do you see each student as an individual?
☐	☐	Do you forget that boys and girls eat with their eyes?	☐	☐	Do you plan and serve attractive food?
☐	☐	Do you serve "messy" plates (trays with food hanging from the sides or several food items "run together")?	☐	☐	Do you merchandise your food—make it look so inviting that customers cannot resist?
☐	☐	Do you serve unidentifiable menu items, such as "mystery meats"?	☐	☐	Do you place the name of the food and its origin on the outside of the serving counter above the item?
☐	☐	Do you wear plastic gloves for serving and handle pots and pans while wearing them?	☐	☐	Do you use tongs, scoops, ladles, or spoons for serving?
☐	☐	Do you plan dead menus, such as dry lima beans, creamed potatoes, apple cobbler, cornbread, and milk?	☐	☐	Do you plan *NOW* menus, such as spicy pizza, crisp garden salad, golden applesauce, "roll-arounds" (cinnamon roll), and milk?

Customer Test (*continued*)

Yes	No		Yes	No	
☐	☐	Do you serve warm milk?	☐	☐	Do you serve refreshing, icy-cold milk?
☐	☐	Do you serve food on cracked or stained plates or trays?	☐	☐	Do you use soft-colored plates or trays that complement food?
☐	☐	Do you show favoritism and give your favorites larger servings?	☐	☐	Do you serve every child the same-size portions?
☐	☐	Do you permit dirty forks in the fork dispenser?	☐	☐	Are you proud of the shiny, spotless utensils that the customers use?
			☐	☐	Do you learn as many of the students' names as possible?
			☐	☐	Do you wear name tags so the students will know you and your employees?

Managing Image with Staff Appearance

Look in the mirror. What does your appearance say about you? Does it say that you are a professional?

If you were going to serve the president of the United States or a senator or congressman or any other celebrity, would you change anything about your appearance? What would that change be?

Your appearance creates a first impression that lasts. What is your image? Another quick test that you can take will measure your personal

Measuring-Your-Personal-Image Inventory

Look at yourself and *your* habits objectively and evaluate the image that you present daily.

Yes	No	
☐	☐	Do you have a spontaneous, genuine smile?
☐	☐	Do you present a we-care-about-you attitude?
☐	☐	Do you wear clean, wrinkle-free uniforms daily?
☐	☐	Does your uniform fit like a professional's—neither too big nor too little?
☐	☐	Do you participate in a "team look" for your school?
☐	☐	Do you avoid safety pins showing, missing buttons, and sagging hems?
☐	☐	Are your shoestrings kept white?
☐	☐	Do you have your shoe heels repaired or replaced *before* they get that "run-down" look?
☐	☐	Do you avoid socks that show and hose with runs?
☐	☐	Is your hair completely covered with a net?
☐	☐	Is your hair squeaky clean and nicely styled?
☐	☐	Are your hands and fingernails clean?
☐	☐	Do you leave all jewelry at home except your watch and your wedding band?
☐	☐	Do you use combs, makeup, nail files, etc., *only* in the restrooms and never in the kitchen?
☐	☐	Do you keep your hands off your hair and face?

If you answered "yes" to every question, you present an excellent image. If you answered "no" to some, figure out how soon you can turn that negative into an affirmative.

image. After you have finished and scored 100 percent, see how your staff members rate themselves on the same test.

Managing Image with Staff Skills

Your professional skills show in the way that you relate to other staff members and to your customers. They show also in the way that you prepare food that is seasoned "just right" and the way you serve food. Hot foods should be too hot to handle. Cold foods should be icy cold. Serve with your hands *only* the foods that you eat with your hands. Your skills show in the way you seek opportunities to update your skills and glow with pride when you talk about your profession and when you serve customers.

Employees in school foodservice programs are true professionals when they keep an open mind for ideas to improve programs. The actions of the staff must say with each meal served: "We care about you." "We are delighted you are eating and enjoying our food." "We are proud to be in the School Foodservice Program." "We are proud of the food we serve."

Your skills are your professional tools. When those tools become rusty and dull, the food products that you turn out will show it. When your skills of food preparation, service, and merchandising are sharp, your customers (students) will benefit first, your program will benefit next. Our profession will feel the effects as well.

Managing Image with Speed and Efficiency of Service

Who wants to wait in any line ten minutes or more? The length of time that a customer must wait in line often ranks above the quality of food in determining whether or not students buy a school meal. The manager must organize the serving line to serve, rapidly without bottlenecks and without sloppiness. Generally, elementary schools can serve ten to twelve meals per minute, middle schools can serve eleven to thirteen meals per minute, and high schools can serve twelve to fifteen meals per minute. In short-order lines with exact change or tickets, cashiers can serve up to eighteen persons per minute.

The employees who serve on the line should be selected very carefully. They should display a genuine smile, be coordinated and move with a systematic rhythm, and be able to serve rapidly with both hands. Research has shown that two people who use both hands for serving can serve as fast as four people on a serving line. When four people are on the serving line, each one tends to use only one hand for serving.

Research has also shown that employees assigned to specific serving positions on a regular basis are more efficient than those employees who are rotated through all positions. Although foodservice staff need to know about all the jobs that have to be done, no one can be an expert in all operations.

When you as the manager need to do a "people inventory" related to the serving line, use the accompanying lists to assess how you are succeeding.

Here are some ways to please with ease in the lunchroom.

- Greet each student with a smile.
- Appear ready to serve the students.
- Serve food quickly and attractively.
- Serve with the hands only foods that will be eaten with the hands.
- Serve hot foods too hot to handle. Serve cold foods icy cold.
- Answer student questions about food honestly and to the best of your ability.
- Keep the line moving, but do not make the students feel rushed.
- Accept student comments graciously, evaluate them, and take appropriate action.
- Learn as many students' names as possible.
- Dress, look, and act like a professional team.

And then there are some things *not* to do on the serving line.

- Do not stir food unnecessarily.

- Do not put fingers on the food contact surface of serving utensils.
- Do not serve food that is not up to standards.
- Do not serve a portion of food and then remove part of it.
- Do not handle pots, pans, etc., while wearing plastic gloves.
- Do not cough or sneeze over food.
- Do not touch nose, rub eyes, or scratch any part of the body.
- Do not wipe hands on apron or sides of uniform or anything besides a clean towel provided for that purpose.
- Do not chew gum, taste food, or drink anything while at the counter.
- Do not shout orders from the serving line to the kitchen.
- Do not stand with back to serving line.
- Do not try to settle a controversy with another employee or with a customer while serving.

Managing Image with Customers and Community

The school foodservice program is a people-centered program. If it is to be successful, the customers and the school community must see it as "their program." They must claim ownership with pride. The relationship that the manager and her staff have with the customers and the community can determine the degree of success of the program. A good manager must

- Accept responsibility as a part of the educational team in the school
- Take pride in being a professional who has special skills for serving young people
- Ask for suggestions for improving the program
- Involve customers in planning menus and introducing new foods or menu items

- Respond with a smile to all requests, regardless of whether or not the request can be granted; it is important not to feel "put upon"
- Accept criticism graciously, and use it to improve the program, and never become defensive!
- Relax, talk with customers informally, and enjoy serving customers—sincerity pays big dividends
- Remain calm, confident, and stable: a professional tells it like it is, but only after taking time to think and responding courteously but firmly

A good way to develop support for your program in the school community is to establish a Nutrition Advisory Council among the students. When the students are given a piece of the school foodservice action, managers can gain the kind of student support that will have long-term benefits for foodservice in their schools. Students can be involved with menu planning and with promoting nutrition to their classmates.

Organizing a Nutrition Advisory Council (NAC)

1. Discuss the possibility of a Nutrition Advisory Council with your principal and foodservice director.
2. Discuss the factors involved with an interested teacher who will act as cosponsor (guidance counselor, home economics teacher, physical education teacher, or other interested faculty member).
3. Determine the maximum size of the committee.
4. Decide on the most effective way to organize a council. Some of the organizational patterns that have been effective are:
    (a) Each homeroom elects one student to serve on the council. (In a very large high school, this method may result in a committee that is too large to function effectively.)
    (b) A school election is held, and the student body votes on a specific number of students to represent each grade level. Students may campaign to be elected.

(c) A student organization may appoint or elect a committee to serve as the Nutrition Advisory Council for one year. Council membership could be rotated among the various clubs on a yearly basis.

(d) The student council may appoint a Nutrition Advisory Council for each school year.

(e) Each club group may appoint one representative to serve on the council.

5. Officers should be elected for the council. These should include a president, vice-president, secretary, treasurer, and reporter.

6. Choose specific projects that meet the current needs of the student body.

7. Submit project plans to the principal for approval before implementing them.

8. Decide who is responsible for followup.

9. Evaluate the success of each project or activity when it is completed.

10. Encourage the students to plan programs that improve their knowledge of nutrition. Involve local people, resource people to emphasize good nutrition—an Extension advisor, doctor, dentist, and so forth.

ACT (Activities for Customer Testing)

Customer testing can take a number of different forms. You will find that with your customers' assistance, your program can be on a solid footing. Enlist help with menu planning, morale-boosting activities, and nutrition-education activities. You will be pleased with the response.

MENU PLANNING

- The manager may meet once a month with a small group of students to plan menus.

- The student body may vote on favorite foods from a ballot listing foods that could be served on the menu.

- Each homeroom may plan one day's menu. The manager should furnish the information and materials needed and visit the classroom if possible.
- The manager should listen to students' comments, evaluate criticism, and use it wisely.
- Students may serve on a tasting panel to select new foods and recipes for the menu.
- Students may help name new recipes.
- Student interest may be created through contests that activate the imagination of the manager.

Operation Uplift

- Students may decorate the cafeteria to appeal to their age group.
- Clubs may make wall hangings of their emblems and display them in the cafeteria.
- School music groups may provide entertainment during mealtime on special days.
- Student groups may assume the responsibility of keeping the cafeteria attractive during meals. They can encourage other students to return used trays, pick up paper, and clean tables.
- Students can display art and crafts on the walls. Displays should be changed monthly. Space may be assigned to clubs and classes.
- Room dividers may be used to make dining room groupings. They may be suspended from the ceiling or placed on the floor, and they will also baffle the noise.
- Bulletin board quickies can be posted. Clubs may prepare bulletin boards with short nutritional facts or seasonal inspiration. Bulletin boards should be changed at least every two weeks.
- Films or slides may be shown and repeated continuously during mealtime.
- The art club may sponsor an art exhibit featuring pictures of food.

Improving Food Habits

- Students, with the help of the foodservice manager and an interested faculty member, may survey the student body to determine its food habits, using a twenty-four-hour recall of all food eaten. Students may be able to complete this study in the homeroom. The results should be published in the school paper.

- Free pamphlets about good food habits may be furnished to students in the cafeteria. A "Nutri-Corner" may be provided to display materials.
- Students may write stories about the school foodservice and how it contributes to their good nutrition.
- Films that promote good food habits may be provided for club meetings or programs.
- Clubs should be involved in having "Around the World Days" in the cafeteria. The school foodservice department should work with students and the social studies teachers in planning menus typical of other countries. Club members should decorate the cafeteria and provide atmosphere and entertainment.
- Color-coded food groups and approximate calorie counts of food may be posted on the sneeze shield in front of the food (example: brown, yellow, green).
- Facts about specific items may be posted or published. Example: _____ eggs used this week; _____ pounds of ground beef used this week; _____ half pints of milk used this week; _____ rolls used this week.
- Foodservice recipes may be reduced to family proportions and made available to students.

Reaching Out

High school students who are interested in good food habits may

- Work with elementary school students to teach good food habits
- Visit a nursing home during mealtime or volunteer on a regular basis to help feed patients
- Teach needy families how to prepare and serve foods, use donated foods, and provide a pleasant mealtime experience
- Volunteer to work in a hospital to help feed patients (especially children) and to visit during mealtime. (This may be arranged through auxiliary hospital personnel.)

"Selling" your students on the idea of "buying" into the school foodservice program through a Nutrition Advisory Council will reach one very important group of customers. Another equally important group is your community. Without parental support and that of the rest of the taxpayers, a school foodservice program can be a lost cause.

You, as manager, need to polish up your image for the community to see and appreciate. How? Start with your PTA. Attend a PTA board meeting and let them know who you are and what you are doing for their children. Help with "high-visibility" refreshments at a meeting. You can ask them to publish *creatively* written menus in their newsletter, along with some brief nutrition facts. Beat your own drum!

Contact the food editor of your local newspaper if your town has one. If not, contact the editor or special-features reporter. During National School Lunch Week in October, invite them to lunch. If they cannot make it, take a treat to them. They will remember you! When you have those special menu days, let your local media people know about it. Human interest stories that present "good news" always appeal to editors or television producers who have lines to fill and minutes to film.

You will never know whether it will work until you try!

And, since you are undoubtedly a member of the national professional food service association (the American School Food Service Association, 4101 E. Iliff, Denver, CO 80222), you should have enough information available to make you one of your school's experts on child nutrition. Do not shy away from this important responsibility. It is an opportunity to tell the school foodservice story as it should be told. You *and* your assistants should be members of your state and local associations, as well as the national organization.

Questions and Answers

Below are answers to some of the most-often-asked questions about school foodservice:

1. *What is the School Foodservice Program?* The School Foodservice Program is a national nutrition program for students. Lunches are planned to provide at least one third of the stu-

dents' daily food needs as determined by the National Research Council. The lunch pattern is specified by federal regulations. It includes milk, meat or meat alternate, at least two fruits and/or vegetables, and bread. The portions are adjusted to meet the food needs of young people. The average lunch contains about 850 calories.

2. *What are the qualifications of a foodservice manager?* Managers are required to have a high school education or equivalent and foodservice courses such as Overview of School Foodservice, Nutrition, Menu Planning, Food Preparation, and Management. They must keep skills updated through in-service and regular managers' meetings. Training classes and in-service programs also are made available to all school foodservice personnel.

3. *Who supervises the school food and nutrition program?* Local Level: The principal in each school is responsible for the school foodservice program, just as he or she is responsible for all areas of education in the local school. System Level: The Director of School Foodservice Programs coordinates activities, interprets regulations and policies, monitors and evaluates menus, and provides training and on-site supervision. State Level: School Foodservice sections in the states' Departments of Education administer the program, provide technical assistance, and evaluate the program on a regular basis. Federal Level: The United States Department of Agriculture (USDA) is the parent agency for the School Foodservice Program. It interprets laws, issues regulations, audits programs, monitors data, evaluates procedures, and provides guidance to local school systems through each state's Department of Education.

4. *How are meals financed?* Student meals are financed with student payments and federal/state reimbursements. In addition to the cash reimbursement for students' meals, the

Did you ever notice that freezers that work perfectly well for years suddenly decide to give up the ghost on a Friday afternoon just after you have received a shipment of commodity ground beef?

school system receives USDA-donated foods. Certain indirect costs are paid by the local school system. Adults must pay the full cost of the meal. Federal law requires that the School Foodservice Program operate on a financially sound, nonprofit basis. Any money taken in as "profit" is reinvested in the program, for new equipment and better serving capabilities.

5. *What if a student cannot afford to pay the regular price for the meal?* Parents may apply for free or reduced-price meals for their children. The eligibility of each student is decided in accordance with the approved School System Policy as filed with the state Department of Education. Income and size of family are considered. The anonymity of the student receiving a free or reduced-price meal is protected.

6. *Who plans the menus?* In school districts where central offices do not provide menus, managers in each school plan menus for their schools. They are responsible for keeping the meal pattern within the cost and productivity framework for their schools. Managers also are responsible for participation and plate waste. Each school is encouraged to serve a choice of menus or a choice of foods within the menu. Managers in schools prepare and cook most of the foods on site.

7. *What is the difference between "health foods" and "healthy foods"?* All foods are "health foods" if the body needs the nutrients contained in the foods. Because of the commercialization of the phrase *health foods, healthy foods* is used in school foodservice programs. Eating a wide variety of healthy foods, whether they are labeled "health foods" or are chosen from the foods readily available at the local supermarket, will provide good nutrition.

8. *What influences food habits of young people?* The home continues to be the most significant influence on the food habits of young people. However, the School Foodservice Program plays an important role in developing good food habits. When young people are served a variety of foods, they develop a broader spectrum of tastes. Students are more likely to taste new foods at school if their peers eat them. The appearance of the food invites students "to eat or not to eat."

9. *Why is nutrition education important?* The students should learn the relationship between good food choices and health. They should be able to apply this information outside of school in their everyday lives.

10. *Why should parents and the School Foodservice Program work together?* The teaching of nutrition at home and at school through foods served or classroom activities should be coordinated to reinforce the importance of practicing good nutrition throughout life.

Managing Image with the Appearance of Food

The food served in the school foodservice program must look *so* inviting that the customer's mouth will water when he or she sees it. If the food looks appealing, the customer will taste it. If the food tastes good, the customer will eat it. In food, the appearance creates an image. For example, a green vegetable that is green when it is served, rather than grayish green because of overcooking, will be appealing to customers. Customers will be attracted by simple garnishes, such as sprigs of parsley in a pan of whole-kernel corn or slices of lemon in one corner of a pan of fish fillets. Put foods on the line just before serving—they will appear and will *be* fresher than food that has been set out too soon. Consider how different foods will look next to one another: arranging colorful foods next to brown or white foods can create an appealing image.

Managing Image with Quantity of Food Served

The quantity of food served must be large enough and contain enough calories to fill up most customers. If most customers are still hungry after eating a school meal, their impression is, "The school does not serve enough food," even though the meal does meet all the requirements.

> *Did you ever notice that business is always bad with salesmen?*

The quantity of food served must also look like enough food. If it does not, customers feel that they are not getting their money's worth, and the program image deteriorates.

Attention must also be paid to serving too much food. Serving too much food means waste in most cases. The age of young school foodservice customers must be considered by servers. Children in the primary grades do not require nor do they often want large servings.

Constant attention is needed to determine what foods are coming back uneaten to the dish return area and who is not eating them. A vegetable that is "good" for the customer but ends up in the garbage is useless. Some food waste is to be expected, but knowing your customers as individuals and knowing their food likes and dislikes *before* food is prepared will reduce food waste.

Managing Image by Merchandising Menus

"Come, eat with us today" is the invitation that managers issue as they write menus in descriptive terms, plan special menus focusing on a theme or special event, or do "something extra" in the way of contests and treats.

Descriptive Terms

Descriptive terms make the meal sound so good that customers cannot resist. When menus are published in the newspaper or newsletters to parents, posted in the dining room, or read over public media or the public address system at school, a mental image is created. If customers visualize mouthwatering delights, they are more anxious to buy a meal. And if good, tasty food supports the positive mental image created through the "advertisement" of menus, participation will soar.

Publicized menus are often the first means of contact with customers. Good managers make menus inviting. For example, *crisp tossed salad* creates a positive image. It sounds better and creates a better mental image than just *salad*. Visualize a *steaming hot bowl of school-made vegetable soup.* It issues a better invitation than *soup.* Other examples of descriptive menu wording include:

- Golden-brown french fries
- Buttered whole-kernel corn
- Hot-from-the-oven rolls
- Chock-full-o'-chips cookies
- Creamy, crunchy cole slaw
- Italian cheese pizza
- Char-broiled hamburgers
- Icy cold milk
- Steaming cinnamon rolls
- Spicy Mexican chili
- Crispy fish fillets
- Whipped mashed potatoes with butter
- Golden-fried chicken nuggets
- Crisp and meaty tacos
- Home-style green beans
- Mamma Mia Lasagne
- Deli-style sandwiches
- Juicy fresh peaches

To merchandise your menus with descriptive terms:

- Make a list of inviting descriptive terms and keep it in a convenient place for easy reference.
- Keep your list of descriptive terms updated by reading professional and trade magazines and by observing commercial advertising.
- As menus are planned and prepared for publication, select the descriptive term for each menu item that creates an irresistible mental picture. And remember that color, flavor, texture, and shape are very important in creating the "advertisement."

28 ∞ I Can Manage

Publishing your menus gives you the opportunity to merchandise your program. "Sell" your menus by the way you present them to the newspaper. Use your descriptive terms and list the menu items in this order:

meat/meat alternate

starch (pasta, rice, etc.)

salad

vegetable

bread (Exception: If the bread is needed for completion of main dish, list bread immediately after the meat/meat alternate. Example: Hamburger on warm bun.)

dessert

milk

Note: Menus will always contain meat/meat alternate, fruit/vegetable, bread, and milk. A menu may or may not contain a starch, salad, or dessert.

Special-Feature Menus

Special-feature menus are planned around a particular theme. They are most effective when the entire school is involved—students, faculty, and the school community. Holidays are often the focus of special-feature menus in elementary and middle schools, while athletic events may serve as the theme in high schools. Menus are often related to what is being taught in social studies classes. Costumes are brought from home or borrowed. The foodservice manager and assistants decorate the cafeteria, working with the principal, teachers, and the PTA. It is a lot of work but a lot of fun.

> **Did you ever notice that no sooner do you get the floor mopped than the milkman arrives with enough grease on his shoes to lubricate his truck?**

∞

Your Management Image Is Showing ⚭ 29

An example that has proven popular with many schools is "Pioneer Days." It affords the opportunity to involve older community members, to feature "old-fashioned" menu items, and to dress in costume. Another fun day has been tied to the science-fiction craze. Think what you could do with menus and costumes! To plan a special-feature menu:

- Gather ideas for special-feature menus as you talk with your principal, faculty, or friends.
- Consult with teachers and make a list of special-feature menus that will parallel classroom activities.
- Observe special holidays, sports events, school activities, or commercial promotions.
- Make a file for each special-feature menu that contains ideas for menus, food items, recipes (preparation and/or serving techniques), decorations used (or needed), invitations to special people and the media, publicity ideas or press releases, and student or community involvement.

Make the special-feature menus festive and "interest-catching," and reap the benefits of satisfied customers as you and your staff serve with pride.

Something Extra

Participation lagging? Menus have the "blahs"? Excitement nil? Students hungry after eating lunch? If your answer is *yes* or even a strong *maybe* to any of these questions, consider serving "something extra," especially on days when the meal requirements and nutritional requirements have been met. And when the budget can afford it.

"Something extra" is just that—something that adds a twinkle to the customer's eyes and calories to end hunger pains *after the meal requirements have been met.* Something extra can be very small: A 90 to 100 cut from a sheet cake; a 1½-inch to 2-inch school-made cookie; a #40 scoop of pudding or a taste of pie. Use the open-draw commodities—surplus commodities often available from the Department of Agriculture. Let your state distributor know that you are interested in being notified when these are available for open draw. Increase interest in the program and then enjoy the benefits of providing "something extra."

Contests

You can build interest in your foodservice program with imaginative contests. On a "dress-up day," tied in with a special-feature menu, ask a faculty committee to help determine the winner, who will receive a special surprise—a cookie, an ice cream cup, a pencil, a T shirt—from you and your staff. And how about an Honors Table in the cafeteria with linen and china service for special recognition of students and for special school guests? Have you thought about your own "Gong Show"? Set a timer at random intervals as a class comes through the line. When the timer goes off, the student paying the cashier at that moment gets the special, nutritious "treat" of the day.

Not only does merchandising add more customer interest in your program, but it can also start the creative juices flowing among your staff members. When you excite people, it is like throwing a rock in a pond. You never know what the ripple effect will be. If you have fun with food, you will have increased participation by both students and adults.

Managing Image with Cleanliness and Appearance of Facilities

Sparkling-clean facilities, perhaps enhanced by displays of student artwork, invite customers to participate. Sparkling-clean facilities mean

- No buildup of grime around walls and under equipment
- Smudge-free windows (serving counter, manager's office, back door, etc.)
- No crumbs anywhere (in serving-counter wells, under the counter, on pan racks, in pass-throughs, or in ovens)
- All splatters cleaned up immediately, including messes around mixer

- No spill-coated shelves anywhere
- No gunk in can openers or around knife handles
- No hidden leftovers in the slicer
- No mold or spoiled food in the refrigerator
- No collection of stuff on the backs of trays and in bowls
- No greasy film on anything
- No leftover odors
- No visitors with more than two legs in storage areas
- No clogged filters over production areas

If you do not already have a checklist that you use to take your cleanliness inventory, we urge you to make one. You can be sure that the health department inspector has one when he comes to visit. We do not advise eating off the floor, but it still holds true that the floor should be so clean that you *could* eat off it.

Managers, Take Notice!!!

Notice what students are or are not eating. That is your responsibility. If students are returning 50 percent or more of any one menu item: (1) "Take a taste" to be sure that it is seasoned "just right" and the temperature is "just right" when the food *reaches* the customer. (2) Hold a "getting-to-know-the-food" tasting party to spark the students' inquisitive minds and create interest in the food. Find some interesting and unusual facts, "near facts," and/or legends to tell the students, and then let them taste it at the "get-acquainted" tasting party. (3) Serve the menu item as a choice item on future menus. When students help select a food item, they are more likely to eat it. Food only provides nutrition when it is eaten. You cannot afford plate waste.

If participation drops by more than 10 percent (without an unusual number of absentees):

- Look at the trays, bowls, or plates. Do they look so unattractive that students do not buy them? Do any of the menu items look like a "glop" of stuff thrown at the plates? If that is true, be careful with the planning and serving.

- Was a "students' favorite" food included? If not, consider "something extra" for the next time that menu is served.

- Has the menu or a food item joined the "same-old-stuff" category? Be careful about serving the same menu or the same kind of menu more than once a week, unless there are numerous choices offered (some menus and menu items become worn out with repetition).

- Does the menu have contrast? Is there something crisp? Something soft? Do the colors of foods look "happy"?

- Does your staff look like a professional team? Are shoes sparkling clean and polished? Do uniforms show school pride with color and fit? If a school chooses white uniforms and the aprons do not "team up" for a match, serve without aprons. *Avoid a "hodgepodge" image.*

- Initiate a we-care-about-you campaign. Plant a permanent smile on your face, even if your feet are killing you. Nourish it with genuine love and care from your heart. Practice patience. And spread pride and enthusiasm for serving people.

- Image is in the eye of the beholder! Work hard to create a good one so that you never have to worry about rescuing a *bad* image.

Did you ever notice that, when it comes to trying something new to eat, most kids have all the adventurousness of rocks?

Jessie, I Need Help

This was the fourth time in two weeks, and it wasn't like Betty Jo. Not at all.

Miss Jessie was a dream of a manager to work for. Over the years, her assistants had all said so. She was fair. She carried her sense of humor to work nearly every day. She treated everyone the same. She expected a full day's work for a full day's pay, and she never asked anyone to do something that she wouldn't do herself. Of course, she wasn't perfect. She had a temper that, most of the time, she didn't allow to get out of hand. But if you tried to pull a stunt, that was something else. Take one of the new delivery guys; he hadn't known that Jessie went over every delivery with a fine-toothed comb. When she found that she'd been shorted not one, not two, but three items, she asked through clenched teeth how that was possible. She knew her vendors well and they knew her. They never shortchanged Miss Jessie unless they didn't have the food in stock; and if they didn't, they let her know.

The delivery guy started out by being flippant. He didn't get very far. Next he tried the "Why, ma'am, they-must-not-have-put-the-full-order-on-the-truck" routine. Jessie didn't say a word as she reached for her telephone. At that point, the man became belligerent. That did it. Jessie's eyes glittered with rage as she slowly rose, put her hands on her hips, and in a tone of voice that would have cut diamonds, said, "Young man, you will get back in that truck, you will get those shorted items from wherever you have to get them, and you'll be back here in one hour. Is that clearly understood?"

He was close to erupting. But the look in Miss Jessie's eyes changed his mind. He was back in an hour. He never made another delivery to Middleville Consolidated.

Betty Jo walked in the back door at 8:20, twenty minutes late. Edna looked at Josie. Josie looked at Evelyn. Then they all looked at Jessie. But she barely glanced up from stirring the chili in the steam kettle.

Betty Jo said nothing to anyone as she pulled off her sweater, tied on her apron, and went to the walk-in for the salad vegetables. As she came out, Evelyn nudged Josie. Betty Jo had put down the vegetables and was wiping reddened eyes.

A half hour later, with meal preparation in full swing, nobody paid any attention to Jessie when she motioned Betty Jo to follow her out onto the loading dock. Betty Jo wasn't herself. Normally, she was quiet-spoken and cool as a cucumber. She would share laughter, but she never started it. If she had a sense of humor, she kept it to herself. In the last month, however, she had not even shared laughter. Betty Jo was withdrawn and her work was haphazard. Where before there had been pride, there was now only a vacuum. Jessie had worked with her for three years, yet she still felt that she didn't know Betty Jo. At lunch she had sat with Betty Jo a number of times and tried to draw her out—without much luck. Of her three children, only one was still at home, and he had finished school and was working. Her husband was a carpenter and was home much of the time. Betty Jo needed to work.

As she stepped out the back door onto the loading dock, Betty Jo was sullen. "Betty Jo, this is the fourth time . . ." That was as far as Jessie got.

Betty Jo lashed out angrily with words that were too loud. "I knew you were laying for me. Edie and Josie have been late before, and you've never called them out. But then, they're your pets, aren't they?"

Jessie didn't answer. The silence lengthened. "Well, aren't they?" Betty Jo demanded.

"Betty Jo, as I started to say, you've been late four times in the last two weeks. Now, if something is wrong at home, and you need . . ."

Too quickly, Betty Jo retorted, "What happens in my home is none of your business as long as I do my . . ."

"Your work?" Jessie said firmly, completing her sentence. Betty Jo's mouth became a straight white line. She turned her head away from Jessie and stared at nothing.

"It's not just your being late, Betty Jo." Jessie spoke quietly and then waited. She waited until their eyes met. "Are you satisfied that you've been doing the best job that you could have done these past few months?"

"What's been wrong with my work? If you mean that mess with the cookies . . ."

Jessie shook her head slowly. "No, not that."

"Then what?" Betty Jo asked. Some of the anger was gone, but the belligerence was still there.

"Have you been treated fairly here, Betty Jo?" Jessie asked.

"Well, sometimes you . . ."

Jessie quietly interrupted. "Have you been treated fairly? Your work schedule, your kitchen assignments, your cleanup jobs?"

The reply came slowly. The belligerence was gone. The voice was dead. "Yes," she answered. "I won't be late again." She turned to go.

Jessie gently laid a hand on her shoulder and spoke. "Just

a minute, Betty Jo. It's more than being late. We both know that. Something is happening that is affecting your work. And when your work is affected, this team's work is affected too. Whatever it is, perhaps we can make some changes here to help you out."

For the briefest moment, the stirring of anger was there. Then it died. Betty Jo sighed again, and then she smiled wanly. "Jessie, I'm really sorry. For what I said and for being late." Her voice was quiet. The eyes were no longer hostile. They glistened as she said, "Jessie, I need some help, but I've just been too proud to ask for it."

Jessie put her arm around Betty Jo's waist as they moved toward the kitchen. "Let's work together today, Betty Jo. I'll betcha we can lick this."

And they did. With a little rescheduling and a lot of understanding.

Where Are You Coming From?

Professional management is a phrase that can be said other ways. In too many cases, people think *professional* applies only to someone with a college degree—doctors, lawyers, teachers, ministers. We consider someone a professional if his or her work shows *superior performance on a continuing basis.* That means he or she is less concerned about whether there are initials after his or her name and more concerned about the *quality* of the job that he or she is doing.

The word *management* has been used and overused to describe everything from listmaking before you go to the supermarket to the president's act of running the country. The focus of the term in this book is somewhere in between those definitions. To be exact, there are three senses involved in the kind of management that we are talking about: *common, business,* and *people.*

The only common thing about common sense is that it is so uncommon—except when it comes to ourselves. Consider for a moment that when we accuse someone of having no common sense, it is usually because (1) they do not agree with us; (2) we cannot understand what they are talking about; (3) we think they are making a mountain out of a molehill; (4) we are convinced that they are too full of themselves or something else; or (5) all of the above.

Business sense is common sense with regard to money—how it comes in and where it goes out. Everyone from the president of IBM to those of us with house payments, car payments, and youngsters in college needs business sense. How much do you have coming in and can you increase it? How much is going out and can you save anywhere? That is what business sense is all about.

Common sense and business sense are important, but if you do not have people sense, you are lost. People are the most important resource in any operation, and if you do not know how to work with them or like to work with them, do not get into management. If you are now in management and do not value the people you supervise above every other resource you have, do a favor to everyone involved. Make a career change!

Qualities of Professional Managers

- Professional managers have a keen sense of responsibility. They evaluate each opportunity objectively and make decisions based on facts. They make the decisions and do things without being told, and they encourage their staff to do the same. It is not what managers know about managing that counts. It is what they do. Taking initiative marks the difference between an effective manager and an average one. Good managers are self-starters. If there is a question about whether or not someone has the authority to act, a good manager points out the problem to the appropriate person, makes a recommendation for solving the problem, and asks for approval to proceed. Good managers recognize when something needs to be done and then go ahead and do it.

- Professional managers develop new ideas and methods without waiting to be prodded. They anticipate needs.

- Professional managers have a strong sense of urgency about getting started and getting jobs finished, and they encourage this same initiative and sense of urgency with their staff.

- Professional managers measure people by how much they get done—the results—not by the motions they go through or what they say.

- Professional managers have confidence. Confidence comes from knowledge, preparation, and practice. Confident managers build confident staffs.

- Professional managers are dependable. They are there when they are needed. They will stand behind employees and the program. They are on the job every day, finish what they start, and are willing to go that extra mile. Dependable managers do not need to advertise the fact; it is visible in what they themselves accomplish.

- Professional managers have a good sense of timing. They know the right thing to do, at the time it has to be done, and they get it done without being told. They understand that there is a "right time" to do everything, and they do not need to be reminded that deadlines are approaching.

- Professional managers express opinions tactfully. Sometimes the manager's opinion may not be the same as the opinion of the principal or supervisor, but once the decision is made, a good manager works diligently. Winning a verbal battle is less important than getting the job done.

- Professional managers keep score for themselves. They set practical goals for their program and know how they are doing from day to day, week to week, month to month, and year to year. They aim high enough to be challenged but not so high that it is impossible to reach their goals.

- Professional managers recognize the tremendous gains in good will that come from giving credit for a job well done. They want their employees to "shine." They know that effective employees reflect good management.

- Professional managers are concerned about the welfare of their employees. They do not use employees for self-gain, nor do they manipulate them.

- Professional managers are eager to improve their skills of leading and managing people. They know that outdated skills can destroy programs.

- Professional managers know that motives show through action. They know that the right motives are more important than the right moves, that people's motives *cannot* be concealed, that

Did you ever notice that just about the time you begin to understand how to complete a pesky reporting form, it gets changed?

employees respect those who are honest, truthful, and straightforward. Managers cannot fake these attributes for long. They must come from the heart. Sincerity cannot be turned on and off like a water faucet. Building mutual trust takes time and effort.

- Professional managers have sincerity and integrity. These qualities show; managers do not have to advertise them. They soon become common knowledge to everyone. Nor can insincerity be hidden, disguised, or covered up, no matter how competent or professional a manager may be.
- Professional managers deserve good will and high esteem from employees. They are recognized for what they are and not for what they want to be. Employees immediately become suspicious when managers go out of their way to be nice to them.

Anyone who has managed any staff or project knows that the list of the traits of a professional manager could go on and on. However, you will make it as a manager if you remember "The Magic Seven" rules in the accompanying chart.

People Inventory

In foodservice, we spend a lot of time worrying about inventory, and rightfully so. When someone mentions "inventory," your first thought probably is food.

For many foodservice managers, inventory means the food that is on hand in storerooms, freezers, and refrigerators. Of course, without that food, managers would be hard pressed when students started through the serving lines. However, another inventory that is even *more* important is the *People Inventory*. The greatest foodservice cost is labor, and that labor is provided by the manager and the assistants. The best foodservice program is one in which people function as part of a productive team, where they enjoy working with each other, feel a personal sense of satisfaction for the job they do, and seek to improve themselves.

You are among the favored few if your program fits that description. If it does not, there are some steps to take to try to attain that status. The first step needs to be taken by the person in charge, the manager. When the manager is productive, chances are very good that the other people in that operation will be productive too.

The Magic Seven

1. Derive satisfaction from achieving *with* people.

2. Take pride in developing strong, ambitious employees.

3. Operate programs within defined parameters (budget, productivity standards, meal patterns).

4. Keep skills updated.

5. Help employees grow professionally.

6. Laugh at yourself before you take yourself too seriously. Laughter is an excellent safety valve when tensions are high.

7. Take pride in serving young people.

The chart on page 42 gives characteristics of productive and nonproductive managers. No one will grade you on these characteristics, but see which ones apply to you. You have nothing to lose by being completely honest. And you will be able to evaluate your own productivity and see where you need improvement.

Connie Firm is a nationally recognized management expert based in Schaumberg, Illinois. She has her own consulting firm and often gives training sessions in connection with the American Management Association (AMA). At one AMA seminar, she made some observations about managers that are applicable to school foodservice managers.

Managers are people, and, like everyone else, each one is unique in characteristics, in attitudes, and in management techniques. An important part of deciding "where you are coming from," of doing a management inventory of yourself, is to understand the kind of person you are when it comes to dealing with other people. Building on your strengths is one key to improving your management ability. Knowing your weaknesses and keeping them out of your management decisions is another way. When you can objectively look at your own strengths and weaknesses and then at those of your co-workers, you will be taking a giant step toward ensuring the kind of working climate that makes for a healthy and productive program.

Characteristics of Managers

Productive Managers	Nonproductive Managers
Spend most of their time in actual supervision	Spend most of their time working in the kitchen
Are people-centered, concerned with employees' interests and attitudes	Are productivity-centered, concerned with *things*
Spend time planning	Spend little, if any, time planning
Have a positive attitude and an inspirational approach	Have a negative attitude with an "it-won't-work" approach
Evaluate employees on performance	Evaluate employees' performance using personal biases
Speak highly of employees	Have very little good to say about employees
Supervise with ease, poise, and confidence	Are temperamental and inconsistent
Ask for ideas and suggestions from employees	Ignore ideas and suggestions from employees
Know how to judge the quality of food by customers' standards	Make excuses when someone complains about the taste of the food

The DISC Analysis

In his book *Integrative Psychology,* William M. Marston identified a *4-Factor Behavioral Model.* He characterized four types of people in terms of how they handled decision making and working with other people. The labels in his model are: Driving (D), Interpersonal (I), Stable (S), and Conforming (C).

All of us have these factors in our personalities, but one of the factors is usually dominant in each of us. When you can take an honest personal inventory and know what your "hot" and "cold" buttons are, you have made the first step toward deciding how to work best with co-workers. The next step is to ask co-workers to make the same kind of personal inventory. Then sit down with them and figure out how each person's strengths can contribute to the team and its work. Most good managers do this by instinct. But how many times have you said, or heard someone say, "I just don't understand (her) (him)!" Knowing personality types and applying that knowledge in management is one way of gaining that understanding.

Let us take a closer look at just what DISC means.

D = DRIVING PERSONS

An individual whose personality characteristics fall mostly in the *D* (Driving) category:

- Makes decisions
- Tackles problems
- Manages a program well
- Is active
- Carries a heavy workload
- Can operate under pressure
- Can apply pressure to others
- States opinions
- Is a self-starter
- Likes competition
- Will "level" with you

Do you fit this description? Have you ever met someone like this—someone who wants challenges, likes to have authority, and prefers different and difficult assignments? If you are managing a Driver, the following are some ways to get the most out of your working relationship.

- Be clear, brief, and to the point.
- Present your facts in a logical order.
- Ask specific questions.
- If you disagree, take issue with the facts, not with the person.

- Support and persuade by referring to objectives and results.
- Exude competence.
- Do not ramble on.
- Do not cloud the issue or ask useless questions.
- Do not come in with a ready-made decision.
- Do not put your disagreements on a personal basis.
- Do not direct or order a Driver.

I = INTERPERSONAL PERSONS

An individual whose personality characteristics fall mostly in the *I* (Interpersonal) category:

- Is popular and likes to be liked
- Has confidence, shows it, and gives it
- Generally maintains an optimistic outlook
- Can motivate other people
- Has considerable power to persuade

A highly Interpersonal (high *I*) type of person wants recognition, a good place to work, a chance to motivate people, and the ability to be free of too many controls and too much detail. If you lean toward being Interpersonal or work with someone who is, below are some things to keep in mind.

- Leave enough time for socializing, for "idea" sharing, particularly where people issues are concerned.
- Keep details to a minimum when possible and keep on hand a good supply of "turn-on" ideas.
- Challenge them to try out sound ideas and let them know you appreciate them.
- Do not be cold or tight-lipped.
- Do not set down hard-and-fast rules and expect a high *I* to stick to them to the letter.
- Allow time to dream as long as that time comes to an end and you can agree on expected results.

S = Stable Persons

An individual whose personality characteristics fall mostly in the S (Stable) category:

- Can be counted on to be as steady as a rock and dependable
- Will take a job and go for tenure
- Works hard, often with routine matters
- Makes both a good teacher and a good student
- Has considerable patience, particularly when it comes to listening

Stable types need security and want to be in a boat that does not rock too much. They tend to look for areas of specialization and expect to be recognized for their knowledge and their contribution to the group effort. They seek friendship from their boss.

It is important to keep in mind the following suggestions regarding Stable types.

- To show interest in them as people having personal and professional goals.
- Be nonthreatening when you let them know what is expected of them.
- Work with them casually, assuring them that their contributions matter.
- Do not be too demanding or abrupt. Do not push them into a corner, or they will clam up on you.
- Let them know that you will support them on agreed-upon goals, but do not change the game or the rules on them.

C = Conforming Persons

An individual whose personality characteristics fall mostly in the C (Conforming) category:

- Is "brass tacks" all the way. This type of person is almost always well prepared, systematic, and thorough.
- Maintains good records and likes to keep them that way

- Can smell trouble coming and avoids it at almost any cost
- Has a good grasp of detail, plans well, and is technically competent

Highly Conforming (high C) persons need security and stability and support from their boss. They function best when they feel that they have control of their work and know exactly what they are supposed to do. They are good team members.

Remember the suggestions below when dealing with Conforming types.

- Deal with them in specifics, presented in a straight-from-the-shoulder way.
- Do not rush them, but agree on a step-by-step plan to reach goals.
- Take your time with them and do not appear disorganized. Be slow, firm, and methodical.

To sum up: Be aware of yourself and of the people you work with. Use the DISC system to assess yourself and your staff. When you have that awareness and apply it directly to supervising people and making decisions, you will make a difference in your program's overall effectiveness. Adjust to people's styles of handling assignments, capitalize on their strengths, and know yourself. If you do, you will see a significant difference in your program's productivity level.

Positive and Negative Personal Traits

Another equally important part of the people inventory has to do with the traits that determine whether a manager is positive or negative. Take another look at yourself. In the accompanying chart are ten positive managerial traits and ten negative ones. If you give yourself a ten in either column, you have problems. If you give yourself a *positive* ten, you may well be a candidate for sainthood. If you end up with a *negative* ten, you are going to need more help than you will find in this book.

Most of us, if we are honest with ourselves, will fall somewhere in

Management Traits

Positive Traits	Negative Traits
M—Motivating employees to perform each task to the best of their abilities	M—Monopolizing every conversation and taking full credit for all successes
A—Anticipating, looking ahead with a work plan that will lead the foodservice program to greater heights	A—Adjusting, correcting errors and oversights caused by poor planning and thoughtlessness
N—Negotiating a point of view to reach a consensus of opinions before taking action	N—Nagging or annoying by continual scolding, fault finding, and complaining
A—Activating carefully planned programs	A—Antagonizing people by opposing changes in improvement and imposing personal prejudices
G—Gracious in accepting compliments and genuinely interested in the welfare of employees and customers	G—Grouchy, complaining, and grumbling about minute details
E—Enthusiastic, radiating warmth, and inspiring others to share the responsibility for providing an outstanding foodservice program for every child	E—Enforcing an autocratic rule by the strength of a position title
M—Magnetic in the sense of drawing out the best in each employee	M—Mandating and decreeing "thou shalts" and "thou shalt nots"
E—Evaluating programs to determine progress and to chart future courses	E—Evading issues and avoiding answers by being clever or dishonest
N—Neutral in order to evaluate each situation objectively	N—Narrow and prejudiced, with a limited outlook
T—Tactful, having a delicate perception of the right thing to say or do without creating bad feelings	T—Tantalizing by arousing enthusiasm for building an outstanding program and then failing to follow through, causing disappointment and anguish

between. It is that "between" that determines where you need to put some time to improve your management ability. Your final score—subtracting your negative traits from your positive traits—is not as important as focusing on the negative traits that can be turned into positive ones.

Is there anyone who does not have some of these negative traits along with the positive ones? Is there anyone who, in doing a personal inventory, cannot identify at least one trait that cannot be improved?

Answering *yes* to these two questions will not bring about a change in us. To make a positive change, we need to keep those trait evaluations handy and ask ourselves often how we are doing with the aspects that need improvement. The best time to do that, we have found, is when we are faced with making a decision.

Making Decisions

All managers have a need to decide on a course of action. Often these decisions have to do with how to use resources most wisely. The most vital resources in foodservice are people, and managers must make decisions every day that affect the lives and careers of the people they work with. Sometimes inexperienced managers ignore problems and the decisions that should be made about them. Good managers face the problems, accept the responsibility, and decide one way or another. Some decisions have definite answers and some do not. Some decisions will not be the right ones. No one can be right all of the time, but making no decision is often worse than making a wrong one.

Difficult decisions are easier to make if managers

- Are aware of their personal goals and the goals of the program. (You cannot make a decision if you do not know what you want.)
- Recognize that there is a problem or that a decision needs to be made
- Consider each decision separately, one at a time
- Are prepared by knowing the facts and the alternatives
- Know what they do not know

- Are not afraid to ask questions
- Write down the problem and the *real* reason it exists
- Take time to think through all of the possibilities

Time tends to help you see the issues more clearly. Very few decisions must be made instantly. Listen and observe. Brainstorm. Write down every possible solution regardless of how unlikely it is. When the best solution is still not evident, eliminate or mark through the *least acceptable* solution, then the *next least acceptable,* until there are only two possible solutions left. Now weigh the pros and cons of each. (You may actually list the pros and cons for each solution on a piece of paper.) Select the best solution after objectively studying the pros and cons, and make the decision with a strong conviction. Commit yourself to your final decision. Do not be wishy-washy. That will accomplish nothing.

When managers feel good about the decisions they make, employees will react and act with confidence.

Below are some questions to ask when you face a decision.

- What is the goal?
- What is the *real* problem?
- What are all of the possible solutions?
- Which solution is best?

How to Say No

After you have analyzed a problem, decided what your options are, and are ready to make a decision, you will need to know how to say *no* without feeling guilty. A manager's effectiveness can often be measured by the things that he or she does not do, and that may mean saying *no.* Learning to say *no* without feeling guilty requires managers to know their own limitations, evaluate each situation or request on its own merits, and establish priorities.

If you say *yes* and then feel unappreciated or guilty, you are not making clear decisions. Do you say *yes* to unrealistic requests because you are trying too hard to get people to like you? Because you are looking for a favor in return? Because it is "the easy way out"? If the answer to any one of these questions is *yes,* you should practice the art of saying *no* without feeling guilty.

Say *no* if the request

- Is thoughtless, inappropriate, or unreasonable
- Violates your own values
- Is something the person should do for himself or herself
- Is in conflict with system policy or good ethical business practices
- Conflicts with your own priorities
- Commits others against their will

When you say *no,* say it promptly. Do not drag it out. Make your answer clear. Do not feel obligated to justify every refusal. Be calm and assured and do not show anger and impatience.

At one time or another, you are going to find yourself in a situation where a decision has to be made. You have followed all the suggestions for deciding what to do and the answer still is not a simple yes or no. What do you do? Ask for help.

Getting Help

Being an effective manager does not mean that you will always have all the answers. Reasonable people would not expect that. But, whether you are just beginning in management or have gotten your feet wet, it is important to know where you can go for help in making your decisions.

Principals are responsible for the school foodservice programs just as they are responsible for all other programs at school. Do not be afraid to ask them for advice or help on anything that pertains to school

Did you ever notice that some pieces of equipment that you have to use every day are just plain evil?

policy or procedures. Remember that they want you to succeed just as much as you want to succeed. They are anxious to help in any way they can.

If your school district has a foodservice director and some assistants, the central office staff is responsible for interpreting system-level policies, providing technical assistance, and making recommendations for program improvement. Their main objective is to help you and your staff to provide an outstanding foodservice program for the students in your school.

Your staff also wants to provide a good school food and nutrition program. Its quality reflects on them and their ability. They can help you too, so *do not be afraid to ask your staff for help.* You are helping yourself while building the confidence and participation of your staff members. When your staff members know that they can make a contribution to the program, they will take a more active part in program improvements.

If you want and/or need help,

1. Treat others as you want them to treat you. Ask yourself, "Now, if I wanted me to do this, how would I ask myself?"

2. Ask the appropriate person in a courteous manner. Never tell a person in a demanding tone to help you unless you are willing to face the consequences.

3. Tell the person *why* you need the help. Take a few extra minutes to explain why. It will be worth the effort. Without following up with a reason, you are telling the person instead of asking the person.

4. Thank the person for his or her efforts in helping you.

Asking questions and asking for help is not a sign of weakness. It is a sign of interest. It will improve your program.

Are you committed to being a *professional manager* in the best sense of that phrase? Will you tackle an honest inventory of yourself and the people you work with, stressing the positive and eliminating as much of the negative as you can?

You will not find the answers to those questions in this book. The answers are with you. But a few words of advice are in order to sum up this chapter.

- Do not get caught on a "no-win" treadmill.
- Plan ahead. Establish a timetable. Last-minute and "catch-up" activities are frustrating and often inaccurate.
- Do not make a commitment for more than you can do physically or mentally.
- Establish a standard of quality for yourself and your staff and stick to it.
- Follow up. Follow up. Follow up.

> **Did you ever notice that the assistant in your kitchen who refuses to join the professional association brags about the restaurant dinner that she and her husband "stole" for $25?**

My Time Is Your Time

A telephone call had interrupted him just after he had said, "Miss Jessie, we may have a problem." Jessie had a fleeting thought: *So what else is new?*

She was in Ned Perkins's office. He had been the principal at Middleville Consolidated for two years—ever since the addition was built and enrollment doubled. It was a long time since Billy Wilden had asked for that straw and Rita had collected the kids' money. A half smile played across her face. *Good Lord, it had been a long time. Sixteen? No, seventeen years. Where had all those years gone?*

Ned Perkins rolled his eyes toward the ceiling as he continued to listen to his caller.

There was silver in Jessie's hair now, and, where other people had "laugh lines," as she frequently noted, she had just plain wrinkles. She didn't feel like a grandmother, though. And she was one three times over. Her mind began to wander as she tried to recall the date of her youngest grandson's birthday. Was little Timmy born on the seventh or the eighth? How could she forget that? She must remember to borrow Edie's cake-decorating tips. Wonder if that green food coloring is still good. . . .

"Sorry about that, Miss Jessie." Ned was talking, and Jessie quickly focused on his face and his words. "The problem is that with enrollment going up another 150, we're going to have to schedule three lunch periods, and I don't see how we can squeeze more than twenty minutes for each period."

"Good grief," Jessie answered, "that will throw my prep and serving schedules out the window. Not to mention the extra hands I'll need at serving time. I can't afford to add any more permanent assistants, not with benefits costing us what they are."

Ned nodded, but without much enthusiasm. "I'm sure that you'll be able to work it out, Miss Jessie."

"Mr. Perkins, we can work anything out that we have to, but remember that foodservice has to pay its own way, and three lunch periods are going to push us into extra hours that I'm not sure we can afford. But the real problem is going to come when we try to serve that many kids in twenty minutes and still give them time to eat. We're going to have long lines, kids are going to get turned off by those lines, and participation is going to suffer. Without that participation, we can't afford more people on the line. It's as simple as that."

Ned Perkins's brow creased as he squinted at Jessie. "How could you come up with that conclusion when we haven't even put numbers to paper yet?"

Jessie smiled her "why-I'd-be-glad-to-share-that-with-you,-young-man" smile. "Well, Mr. Perkins, last year we averaged eighty-six percent participation with three twenty-five-minute lunch periods. We could do that because we had 150 fewer kids than we'll have next year and five minutes longer to serve them. No one had to stand in line longer than five-and-a-half minutes, regardless of our menu. Increase that waiting time two or three minutes and cut the lunch period by five and that participation will drop like a rock."

Jessie paused for breath and waited for a response. There wasn't any.

"Now, something else about those additional 150 kids and what they will mean to the assistants and me. We can prepare the food in time, and with rescheduling we can put more hands on the line to serve them. But what we're going to be missing are some hands to keep those lines stocked. We can hire some part-time people to solve that problem for us. That will mean additional labor costs, which . . ."

Ned Perkins threw up his hands in mock horror. "Please, Miss Jessie. You're giving me a no-win situation, and that isn't like you. Have you got a suggestion short of changing Middleville's entire schedule?"

Jessie put her thumbnail to her mouth, squinted one eye, and stared over Perkins's right shoulder. Seconds passed. "Well, it seems to me that we had a problem like this four or five years ago," Jessie answered.

"And?" Perkins asked.

"And we added another lunch period and some . . ." Jessie stopped. Ned Perkins had raised both hands and was shaking his head.

"Can't do it, Jessie. We can't split periods. The teachers will never go for it. Just about the time they get a good start, they have to break for lunch, and after lunch they have to spend ten minutes getting their kids back on track."

Jessie nodded in agreement. "That's very true, Mr. Perkins. But what I was thinking about wouldn't split class periods." She had his attention.

He asked, "Wouldn't split class periods? Now how in the world could that work without changing the entire schedule?"

"Mr. Perkins, is that schedule on computer yet?" Jessie asked.

He narrowed his eyes slightly and gave Jessie a lopsided smile. "You know it isn't nailed down yet or we wouldn't be talking about lunch periods. But we still can't change the schedule."

Jessie nodded in agreement. "Mr. Perkins, it seems to me

that we have a couple of challenges. One is to keep our participation high, and to do that we have to keep away from long lines or at least give kids time to eat. Second, we can't afford to load up with more people than we can afford in foodservice."

"And, third, we don't mess with the schedule," Ned Perkins said, grinning. "Right?"

"Well . . ." Jessie began.

"I knew it," he said.

Oh, does he? Jessie thought. *And just what is so sacred about a schedule when kids and service are involved?*

Her thoughts then became words, and Ned Perkins stared. Jessie smiled.

"Mr. Perkins, our first responsibility in foodservice is to students. And I know that that is yours, too. I don't pretend to know class scheduling, but I know something about foodservice scheduling. I need to ask a question that may seem dumb, but I'm going to ask it anyway. Why do those thirty-minute homeroom periods have to be scheduled first thing in the morning?"

Ned Perkins continued staring. Jessie quickly asked, "Is it possible for those classes that would be split by longer lunch periods to be scheduled first thing in the morning and then . . ."

Ned Perkins chuckled softly. Jessie looked puzzled, but he didn't. "You're right, Miss Jessie. The schedule isn't sacred. And you just may have come up with the answer to the problem. I guess I had thought that our kids had to be in their homerooms for morning announcements, but they don't. Son of a gun, it just might work. And you know, we might have a better chance to involve the vocational kids in some club activities that way. And then if we . . ."

Jessie almost whispered her interruption. "Does that mean that we might get thirty-minute lunch periods?"

Perkins smiled broadly this time, and he nodded with as much enthusiasm as relief. "I think you've got it, Miss Jessie. I really think you've got it!"

"Thank you, Mr. Perkins. We'll do the very best job that we can." She rose from her chair and moved toward the door.

"You always have, Miss Jessie. You always have."

And the new schedule worked out just fine.

Have You Got a Minute?

How many times have you been asked, "Have you got a minute?" What did you answer? Chances are that you gritted your teeth, even when you were the busiest, and said something like, "Sure, what can I do for you?" And whatever it was took a lot longer than a minute, right? Now it is time to discuss some alternative responses.

Time Management

Time—or the lack of it—is the topic of conversation every day. We need to learn to manage time—or it will manage us.

Think in terms of minutes and how to manage the minute. One minute is built on another. Managers who develop this skill build each hour with minutes organized in a specific manner. Each of their days is built with hours, weeks are built with days, months with weeks, and years with months. There is no reason to start over every week. Managers must take deliberate steps to make sure that *they* manage time.

Time is an economic resource that is precious and expensive. The more we become aware of time and how we use it, the more valuable it becomes. Time is an asset that we can budget and control like we control other resources, such as food, money, and labor.

It is all too easy for us to accept the *lack of control* over our time that we so often have. Few of us realize the true cost of lost or wasted time. If one of your employees said, "The hundred pounds of ground beef is gone. I don't know where it went," you probably would think you had a theft. But if a person said, "I don't know where the day went," you probably would say, "Welcome to the club."

We all feel that our own time-management problems are unique, but time-management consultants who have worked with many different people in many different occupations agree that the "time robbers" are all similar: telephone calls, meetings, visitors without appointments, paperwork or "busy work," demands by co-workers. Often a closer look will show that time loss results principally from the manager's failures—the failure to delegate, the failure to state priorities, the failure to establish a plan of action or a detailed work schedule—*and from putting things off.*

It can be very difficult and painful to inventory your own use or misuse of time and learn that you are the problem, but the reward for making an inventory of the use of your time is making better use of time. It often eliminates confusion on the job, tension, and the general feeling of being out of control. In addition, it results in more time for long-range planning, evaluation, and training. And you will have more free time for yourself.

Effective managers know where their time goes and where it should go. The only way to know how your time is spent is to analyze how it should be spent and to keep records. In reality, you may not be spending your time the way you think you are spending your time.

Planning Is Essential

Plan what you are going to do by the month. On a calendar, write down the things you *must do*. Then plan your other activities.

Plan what you will do each day. Make a Things-To-Do List. You will accomplish more and become less frustrated and you will not become bogged down with the less important jobs. Allow some time for the inevitable unscheduled situations that occur. As much as 40 to 50 percent of a manager's time should be reserved for emergencies and unplanned time-consumers.

Establish priorities. Make three columns on your Things-To-Do Sheet (have to, ought to, want to) and list each activity in the appropriate category. Or make one list and give each activity a priority number. Recognize that some tasks just cannot be done. There is not enough time or they are not important enough or they do not contribute to your goals. It has been said that the best measure of a manager is the list of things that he or she decides to leave undone.

Make a list of everything you did at work on, say, Monday and another list of everything you did on, say, Wednesday.

Evaluate your two lists by asking yourself

- What am I doing that really does not need to be done at all, by me or anyone else?
- Which of these activities could be handled just as well, if not better, by someone else?
- How is the allocation of time related to my major goals?
- What do I do that wastes the time of others?
- How did the things I accomplished *improve* the school food-service program?
- Is there enough time allocated for planning and scheduling?
- Are certain people neglected?
- Which time-consumers involved crises that have happened before or could have been foreseen?
- Is there a pattern of time wasted or unaccountable time?

Another way to decide whether you are spending your time investment wisely is to do another form of a Things-To-Do Sheet. Instead of recalling activities of a day or two ago, some management specialists urge that, at least once every six months, managers keep a Things-To-Do Sheet that divides each day into hours. One column lists the activities scheduled for each hour. Another column allows managers to indicate the *actual* time that each activity took. A third column allows managers to decide, on a scale of one to ten, just how

Did you ever notice that just when the first student starts through the line, two delivery trucks arrive, the telephone rings, and you snag your pantyhose?

important each activity was in relation to the managers' priorities—based upon department/personal goals, job descriptions, or standards of performance.

Those who make their living by helping good management get better suggest that a Things-To-Do Sheet be kept for at least five working days. This allows a true evaluation of where time is spent that does not advance department/personal goals, of whether there are bad time-consumer habits that need to be broken, and of which jobs managers are doing that could and should be delegated.

Few managers are born with the ability to delegate wisely. In most instances, that ability is acquired with experience, but that learning-by-experience road can be a lot smoother when managers listen to and then apply the experiences of successful time managers.

Managers must recognize that they do not have time to do everything, and that some jobs can and should be delegated to others. Managers who know exactly what they want done and feel secure in their jobs can delegate with ease and confidence.

Two of the biggest problems with delegating responsibilities are (1) overcoming the myth that managers must do more than anyone, or do some of everything in the kitchen, and if they do not, they will lose control; and (2) handling reverse delegation—when employees wait to see whether the manager will do the job (so that they will not have to do it).

Below are several suggestions to help you delegate tasks responsibly and successfully.

- Delegate fully the total job. Stress independence.
- Make sure employees understand how to do the delegated tasks.
- Require your assistants to be organized to handle delegation, and show them how to be organized.
- Avoid options. Be specific.
- Challenge employees to their highest competencies.
- Do not duplicate jobs (do not do any job twice).

The question that applies to both time use and delegation is, "Am I doing the most important job *right now*?"

Even when competent managers discipline themselves to complete

Delegating Responsibilities	
Tasks to Delegate	**Tasks Not to Delegate**
Repetitive jobs	Anything that you cannot define
Details (unless they affect program management)	Executive or decision-making functions
Anything that makes you over-specialized	Disciplinary problems
Anything that makes you under-specialized	Anything that involves sensitive groups

a Things-To-Do Sheet and even when they are successful at delegating important foodservice jobs, they are not satisfied that they are doing the best job that they can with the time available to them. Competent managers keep handy a time-management reminder list to help them remember their priorities. Below is one list that many have found helpful.

How to Manage Your Time

1. *Analyze how you use your time.* Write down in detail in chronological order how you spend your day. Look at your activities and see if you can spot areas where you could have saved time. You may see Parkinson's Law in action: "Work expands to fill the time available." Reflect on the day of the month your paperwork had to be turned in. You organized your day and were able to work *almost* uninterrupted if you finished the day's activities. How many of those interruptions could you have avoided altogether if you had had good production, serving, and cleaning schedules?

2. *Group similar work or activities.* Use to your advantage the routine you establish and the momentum you build up. Finish one job before you begin another. Hodgepodge work habits, dabbling with many unfinished projects, and starting one project before another one is finished will waste time and energy. If you organized yourself to do your paperwork and planning before other employees arrive or after they leave,

would you be able to concentrate better and to work faster and more accurately?

3. *Plan ahead.* Plan a week or more ahead. Decide what needs to be done the next day. That will help you to organize your activities and to group similar activities. Observe deadlines. People work better and more efficiently with deadlines.

4. *Motivate others.* One of the best time-savers is to motivate other people to perform at their highest levels.

5. *Use a work schedule to assign duties, quantities of food to prepare, methods to be used, and so forth.* This is an excellent way to avoid repeating instructions to each employee and to avoid wasting time.

6. *Relax your mind.* Keep a "memory sheet" in a small notebook that you carry with you. When you think of an idea to try or something that needs to be done, write it down. You will feel more relaxed and confident and have less tension, and you will not "crowd out" new and refreshing ideas while you constantly think about what you have to remember.

7. *Avoid duplication.* If you and/or your employees are recording the same information twice, time is being wasted. If employees are recording foods used on one sheet of paper and you are recopying the information into a book or onto another list, time is being wasted. If several employees are doing bits and pieces of a single job and a duplication of efforts occurs, time is being wasted. Ask employees for suggestions for reducing duplication of work and for saving time.

8. *Stop using outdated methods of doing things.* Just because something has always been done a certain way, that is no reason to continue doing it that way. Find the "best time" to do work. Plan interruption-free time. Few people can accomplish as much in twenty segments of ten minutes each as they can in one good, solid hour of concentration. Do the

Did you ever notice that the day after you finally got the steam table repaired the VCM goes on the fritz?

most complicated job first, while you are rested and your mind is fresh. Do the hard jobs first so that you can forget them, and then they will not drain your energy.

9. *Be selective.* Concentrate on doing a few jobs well. Trying to do too many things at once, doing things that are unnecessary, and failing to delegate effectively are three of the greatest thieves of time.

10. *"Waste not, want not" can be applied to time.* When you have a few minutes to wait for something, use that time to make a list of jobs that need to be done, decisions that need to be made, procedures that need to be developed, or projects that you want to do. Time is valuable, so do not waste even a minute.

11. *Be careful with time-killers.* Personal telephone calls and salesmen with wares to sell and/or gossip to share fall in the time-killer category.

12. *Plan for rest.* Schedule an opportunity for you and your employees to pause briefly and refresh, to eat together, to share together and to care together.

Some Guaranteed Time-Wasters

A final caution about time management is that you must keep a careful watch against wasting time. We have some surefire time-wasters for you to watch out for.

- *Deemphasize planning.* Confusion and chaos result.
- *"Garble" communications.* Leave questions unanswered on work schedules. Assume that employees know things. Give directions verbally. Fail to answer questions clearly.
- *Hold "bull sessions."* Discuss the weekend's activities while work goes undone.
- *Arrive late and leave early.* If one employee is an offender, the morale of the other employees plunges and production lags.
- *Be insensitive to problems and hope they will go away.* Managers should be able to "sense" a problem, bring it to the surface, and solve it as quickly as possible.
- *Shuffle paperwork.* Pick it up. Put it down in another stack. Repeat several times and you will wonder where the time has

gone. When you pick up a piece of paper the first time, decide what you are going to do with it and do it *before* you put it down.

- *Procrastinate.* The whole staff will put things off with you. The manager sets the pace.
- *Follow up too much.* Employees will become dependent on the manager. Assign specific responsibilities and let the individual complete the job.
- *Insist on perfection.* It is better to let employees work at a good pace instead of slowing them down to point out that every little job lacks something and is not absolutely perfect.
- *Do not recognize achievement.* Good job motivation will decline, followed almost certainly by the production level.
- *Blame others.* Using a scapegoat will demoralize the staff and create tension and misunderstanding.
- *Create an ulcer atmosphere.* Tension and other negative forces will surely destroy a calm, smooth work flow.
- *Do not display a sense of humor.* One who cannot laugh at himself can be miserable. A smile, a cheerful *good morning,* and the ability to laugh when something is funny is wholesome. And, by all means, laugh *with* people, never *at* them.

Did you ever notice that the vision problems that keep your assistants from seeing the crud on the slicing machine disappear when they open their paychecks?

Edie

Rain fell from a gray sky. Jessie put down the phone and looked out the window without seeing—to the row of pine trees that marched up the side of the hill behind her house. For a long minute she didn't move. When she did, it was to cover her face with her hands. And she sobbed.

Edie was gone. After years of working together and laughing together and sometimes crying together, Edie was dead. Her suffering was over. Thank God for that. *But,* Jessie thought, *why always the good ones?*

"Edie, this schedule of mine just doesn't look right. Take a look at it and tell me what you think," Jessie said, as she sat down across from Edie Lambert to share glasses of iced tea before going home. The rest of the staff had not been gone for very long.

"What do you think may be wrong with it, Jessie?"

"Can't put my finger on it, but I think the problem is with Mary Lou's and Sue's assignments. Am I putting them and the rest of us at cross-purposes there just before serving time?" Jessie asked. She put down her glass and pointed to her tentative production schedule. "Are we going to be running around like chickens with our heads cut off just when we should be having a breather to make sure we're ready for the kids?"

Edie absentmindedly chewed on a hangnail as she studied Jessie's production schedule. "I really don't see how . . ." Edie started to say. Then a smile parted her lips. "Jessie, look at this forty-five minutes here. And this twenty minutes here. Could be that you've got two people doing the same job twice, or darn near it."

Jessie pushed her glasses up on her nose and looked closely. She nodded and shared the smile. "Yes, of course. Now, why didn't I see that when I did it? And, for heaven's sake, why not in the umpteen times I've looked it over?"

Edie laughed. "Well, you've only been doing this for twenty years. Give yourself another twenty and I'll just bet that you'll get it right."

Jessie grinned and slapped playfully at Edie's arm. "Thanks a lot! Who needs enemies when they have friends like you? Just for that, you're going to get to do the job analysis to make sure that you're as smart as you think you are."

Edie pretended shocked surprise that didn't quite come off as she laughed and said, "Do a friend a favor and what do you get? More work! Well, I never!"

"Bet you have!" Jessie said with a smile. Then she added, "Thanks, friend. What would I do without you?"

"Well," Edie sighed, "this place would just fall apart like it did for all those years before you took me on and taught me all I know about this business."

They shared a moment of companionable silence, finished their tea, and pushed their chairs back from the table.

"Oh, I almost forgot," Jessie said. "I had a call last night from Mary Burnham about the state convention. She's in a tizzy over whether or not we have the table decorations ready and whether we'll have favors at each plate."

Edie shook her head and grinned. "How many years now have we handled those? Four? Five? Why don't you call her back and let her know that we're almost finished here with the table decorations and that Jefferson and Cobbs Chapters are well along with the favors."

They stood and headed for the kitchen. Edie chuckled softly and then tried to stifle a giggle. She didn't.

"What?" Jessie asked, infected with Edie's laughter and joining her in it.

Edie laughed aloud. "Oh, I was just thinking of that convention in Nashville when eight of us stayed in the same room because the hotel was so expensive and we had to sleep all over the floor and I got up in the middle of the night...."

Jessie interrupted. Her laughter was deep and full. "And you stepped on Irma's stomach, and she kicked Joanie in the head...."

"And, and..." Edie was giggling almost too much to get the words out. "And Joanie let out that yelp that brought Florence straight up and..."

"And Florence hit the lamp table," Jessie continued, "and knocked it over on Bernice and Mary Lou." By now they were hanging onto each other and wiping tears from their eyes.

Edie let out a whoop. "Ginger was the only one who escaped, and remember what she said when she woke up to all that?"

Jessie could barely speak through her laughter as she interrupted, "She wondered if a man had gotten into the room!"

It was Edie's turn to interrupt, "And when we said 'no' and we all started to talk, she said . . . she said . . ."

Both shook with mirth. Somehow they managed to shout together Ginger's final comment, "Shucks!"

Long seconds passed before they gasped their way back to normal breathing and slumped into chairs to wipe their eyes. Jessie shook her head. "So many good memories to share. It never occurred to me all those years ago when I walked in here and saw this place—it seemed so huge then—that I was starting something more than a job. You all have become another family for me."

Edie nodded. "I know what you mean. I just wanted some pin money and something to keep the loneliness away when the kids had all left home. I couldn't imagine that, at my age and with no education, I could find a career, that I could feel that I had something to give to a team of caring people."

"And you have, old friend," Jessie said as she laid her hand gently over that of her colleague. "And you have. During those first weeks I was sure that you didn't know beans from bananas. And then, almost overnight, you were everywhere around here, pitching in to help someone else when you'd finished an assignment, cleaning some piece of equipment because it was dirty and not because you were asked to, helping new people learn the ropes, going to in-service meetings with us. And always with a joke or a smile. That's what it's all about. Making a job more than a job. Caring and sharing. Gee, I make it sound like you walk on water. And that perfect you're not. Edie, I don't know if I've ever said it to you, but I will. Thanks, Edie. For all of it."

Neither one said anything else for several long moments. Edie's voice was low and hushed when she answered. "Dear friend, it's me who needs to thank you. You took a greenhorn and with patience taught me, with example showed me, with understanding led me from doing jobs to . . . Oh, heck, you know what I mean. I just can't say it very well. I just hope that we can go on for a long time."

"I've got the same hope, Edie. For a long time, the good Lord willing."

Jessie's tearstained face was turned again to her kitchen window. The pine trees were still there. Her silent sentinels. They were there before she came to this place. They would be there long after she was gone. *At least some things are constant,* she thought.

The Lord had had other things in mind for Edie. A malignancy. A lingering death. But there was more than that. Even though she knew that there could be only death at the end of that long road, Edie showed Jessie and countless others the meaning of faith. And dignity. As they watched Edie waste away without complaint or anger or self-pity, they came to realize that greatness is measured not in long-remembered achievements but in long-remembered courage. Could anyone who had known Edie face the inevitable without remembering her example?

The rain had ended. Jessie stirred in her chair and wiped her eyes again. And up on the hill, barely visible at first and then, unmistakably, a shaft of sunlight glistened off pine boughs. Jessie stood and looked to her hill. And toward the sunlight.

The Right Equation

∞

The Right Equation in the school foodservice business is simply stated: Jobs to be done + Professionals who know their jobs = Successful Management.

Competent managers not only use their own time well, but they also are committed to the best use of their assistants' time and talents. No foodservice operation can hope to succeed if there is not a strict accounting for every minute of labor by every employee. That accounting begins and continues with the job analysis.

Job Analysis

A good manager analyzes the amount of work assigned to each employee to be sure that the workload is distributed fairly and evenly. A job analysis is one visual method for evaluating the workload that the manager has assigned.

To prepare a job analysis, the manager should (1) be objective and honest; (2) know approximately how long each job takes; and (3) analyze each job for two or three consecutive days.

Managers may sit down with employees and ask them to supply the information so each employee can see how the job analysis is prepared. They will not feel as threatened if they are asked for input. Depending on the situation, managers may prepare job analyses for employees to evaluate their own job assignments.

A job analysis should contain

- The names of the employees
- The approximate time when each job assigned to each employee should be started.
- The approximate time when the job should be finished
- The number of servings of each menu item (or the amount of food) to be prepared
- Other duties assigned

A job analysis can be conducted when

- Managers observe that one employee appears to be doing more than the others
- One employee has trouble completing assignments
- Managers notice that employees have "free time," that they have not been assigned enough work to keep them busy
- Some employees feel that they are required to do more work than others

A job analysis can be prepared for any segment of the day's work (production or serving or cleanup), or it can be prepared for the total day's work.

Managers have the responsibility to assign employees enough work to keep them fully productive. This requires knowing approximately how much time each job requires. Good managers never routinely say, "Help someone else when you finish your job." However, this does not preclude the manager from asking one employee to help another one. When employees are permitted to "choose" which of the other employees to "help," it is often a friend who may not need as much help as another employee. Brief and simple samples of job analyses for two foodservice assistants appear in the accompanying chart.

> **Did you ever notice that there are never any commodity strawberries?**

Work Schedule

Mary

Start	Finish	Job	Amt./No. Servings
		Make taco filling (USDA recipe # _____)	500 @ 2 oz.
8:30	9:15	Get out tomorrow's meat, place in steam pot, stir to break up	
9:15	10:00	Grate cheese and clean up	15#
10:00	10:15	Add seasoning to meat	
		Water to boil for tea	2 gal.
10:15	10:20	85# ground beef in refrigerator	
10:20	10:30	Chip ice; fill glasses	12
10:30	11:00	Eat lunch	
11:00	11:05	Take taco shells to serving line	3 cases
11:05	12:45	Serve taco shell taco meat cheese	

Helen

Start	Finish	Job	Amt./No. Servings
9:00	10:00	Dice tomatoes with french knife	40#
10:00	10:20	Open corn, season with ½# butter per 3 cans	11—#10
10:20	10:50	Eat lunch	
10:50	10:58	Cook ½ of corn in steamer	
10:58	11:05	Take diced tomatoes to line	
11:05	12:45	Serve tomatoes corn cinnamon roll	

Scheduling

Setting up production, serving, and cleaning schedules that effectively use the time and talents of assistants is another vital part of the manager's role to make sure that the foodservice program is genuinely accountable.

"What's cooking today?" is the question asked in many school kitchens as the clock signals that work must begin. That one question probably costs foodservice programs millions of dollars annually, because some employees spend thirty to forty-five minutes finding out what they are supposed to do, which recipe to use, how much to prepare, and so forth.

If a school has four employees and each employee "spins his wheels," making little progress toward the day's work for only fifteen minutes each day, the school could lose more than $1,000 annually. Since employees' productivity is not utilized fully, the number of meals served per labor hour is reduced, and this increases the labor cost for each meal. This time-consuming wheel-spinning does not have to occur. It can be eliminated by a work schedule, or whatever managers choose to call their preplanned and written assignments. Foodservice programs must continue to compete in today's economy, and as wages climb, production practices must keep pace. Optimum use of funds must be practiced in every school.

Managers must prepare written production, serving, and cleanup schedules that assign employees to complete specific tasks. This does not mean, however, that they should *not* help other employees when they have finished their assigned activities. It does mean that they can take pride in their own accomplishments because they know exactly what is expected of them. It also means that each hour spent on the job is productive and effective.

Production, serving, and cleanup schedules can be as simple or as complex as the manager chooses to make them, but they must tell employees *exactly* what to do. Employees should be able to read the schedules and know exactly what to do without asking questions. All schedules should be posted in a conspicuous place that is accessible to all employees.

Production, serving, and cleanup schedules can accomplish a great deal, but there are some important truths and untruths about them. Some truths are that they:

- Save time and increase productivity
- Create job security
- Reduce fatigue
- Equalize job responsibilities
- Can be evaluated regularly (by managers and employees)
- Stimulate pride and cooperation

- Reduce friction among employees
- Make efficient use of equipment

Some untruths about production, serving, and cleanup schedules are that they:

- Create more work
- Destroy morale
- Cause loss of status
- Prevent or minimize employees' input
- Disrupt the smooth flow of work
- Destroy individuality
- Are not flexible
- Prevent interaction among employees
- Hamper scheduling of equipment

Of course, production, serving, and cleanup schedules *can* fail. This can happen when the need for organized planning is not recognized; when a good, practical, workable schedule is not used; and when employees do not understand a work schedule and/or do not have input into it.

Production Schedule

There is no fail-safe production schedule. It may take several starts to develop the one that best fits a manager's state and school district requirements, the time and talents available, and the manager's previous experience with production scheduling. Make your production schedules a permanent part of your production records.

A production schedule should include

1. Date
2. Menu
3. Employees' names

4. Menu items and food items
5. Recipe(s) to be used
6. Amount to prepare
7. Size and number of servings
8. Time that assignment is to be finished (*if* the exact time is important)
9. Special instructions to be used for preparation and/or serving
10. Special serving or other instructions
11. Serving utensils needed

In some school districts, production schedules also contain

- Unit cost
- Total cost of menu items
- Other data that allow the manager to calculate daily the total amount spent for food, labor, and supplies

The production schedule can also be used to check off food orders and deliveries and to document price quotations.

When scheduling production, we recommend that managers

- Do not always assign employees to work "in pairs"
- Assign two employees to a job *only* when two persons are needed to complete the job
- Designate the first name on a list of two or more as the lead person, who should be responsible for the amount prepared, seasonings, and quality of the product

For a sample, we have selected the production schedule used in Cobb County, Georgia. You may have one that works better for you, but even if you do, you may get some new ideas from this one. Following the production schedule and its accompanying salad-preparation sheet are the instructions for putting it all together.

Sample Production Schedule

Date _____ School _____

Total no. meals served __100__   Manager _____

Person Responsible	Servings No.	Servings Size	Menu Item	Quantity Prepared	Unit Cost	Total Cost
Mary	100	2 oz.	Hot dogs – steamer (10 min.)	13 #	$1.49	$19.37
			Buns – warmer (9 a.m.)	9 doz.	.50	4.50
Susan	100	¼ c.	Cole slaw: USDA recipe			
			Cabbage: chop in VCM	5 #	.30	1.50
			Carrots: chop in VCM	2 #	.25	.50
			Mayonnaise	1 gal.	.90	.90
Dot	100	½ c.	Peaches, sliced	5 10 #	2.25	11.25
Lucy	100		Chef salad base	(see p. 78)	6.89	6.89
Brenda			Eggs, boiled ½s	50	.06	3.00
			Cheese 1 oz.	7 #		USDA
			Ham ½ oz.	4 #	1.49	5.96
	30	2 pckg.	Saltines	60	.05	3.00
Mary			Clean bathroom			
Dot			Sell tickets			
			Milk served with meals & used in cooking		.115	15.53
			Condiments (no. meals x .03)			3.90
			Other costs (no. meals x .05)			6.50
			Total labor cost			25.50
			Total cost of meals			108.30

Did you ever notice that the managers who run the best programs talk about them the least?

Sample Salad-Preparation Sheet

Date _____
Person Responsible _____

Ingredients	Amount Used	Cost per Unit	Total Cost
Lettuce	16 #	.29	$ 4.64
Red cabbage	2 #	.30	.60
Carrots	3 #	.25	.75
Green pepper			
Broccoli			
Spinach	3 #	.30	.90
Yellow squash			
Other ingredients (list):			
Total Cost			$ 6.89

Preparing the Production Schedule

1. List in column 3 each menu item to be served. Write down the food items to be used in each menu item, the recipe number, and any other special instructions.

2. Draw a circle around the vitamin C–rich foods. Draw a line under the vitamin A–rich foods.

3. List in column 2 the projected number and size of servings of each menu item to be prepared.

4. List in column 4 the quantity of food to be prepared as pounds, #10 cans, and so forth. If assistants prepare more or less food, they should draw a line through the original quantity and write in the amount actually prepared. A separate salad-preparation sheet may be attached, as shown in the sample. Be sure to transfer salad-preparation costs to the production schedule and file the forms together.

5. List in column 5 the cost per unit as the cost per pound, #10 can, and so forth.

6. Write in column 1 the name of the person(s) responsible for preparing each menu item. If two or more persons are as-

signed to prepare a menu item, the first person listed should be designated the lead person.

7. After the menu is served, multiply the quantity of food prepared (column 4) by the unit cost (column 5) to determine the total cost (column 6). Note: If food prepared on one day will be served another time during the week, record the total quantity and cost on the day prepared. Post the number of servings served on specific days in a small circle above the menu item. List menu items on each day that they are served. Make a note in the total cost column—"Refer to (day)"—to indicate when the menu item was prepared and costed.

8. Bread (or perhaps buns, as in the sample being used). If purchased bread is served, list the total quantity and cost. if school-made bread is served, multiply the number of servings (meals) by .02 (this can vary) to determine cost.

9. Staples. Record staple commodities (flour, oil, dried milk, and so forth) on the day the bag/can is opened.

10. Complete the bottom portion of the production schedule.

11. Remember that every food or beverage that is prepared should have a place on the production schedule.

Income/Expense Comparison Sheet

Prepare an income/expense comparison sheet each week so that you always know your current financial standing. Use your production schedules to calculate expenses. To obtain weekly income totals, use cash-register tapes and/or forms provided for that purpose by your district.

The Serving Line

It would be difficult to choose which of the following is most important on the serving line: how the line looks to the customers in terms of eye appeal; the attitude of the people serving those customers; the

Sample Income/Expense Comparison
(Elementary/Middle Schools)

1. Multiply # paid student lunches by sale price	600	x	.75	=	$450.00
2. Multiply # paid student lunches by federal reimbursement rate	600	x	.105	=	63.00
3. Multiply # reduced-price lunches by sale price	5	x	.30	=	1.50
4. Multiply # reduced-price lunches by federal reimbursement rate	5	x	.8475	=	4.24
5. Multiply # free lunches by federal reimbursement rate	10	x	1.1475	=	11.48
6. State reimbursement amount					
7. Multiply # paid adult lunches by sale price	50	x	1.30	=	65.00

Total income available (add lines 1 through 7) $595.22

Total expenses for week (Expenses from production schedule) $524.86

Difference $ 70.36

EXPENSES FOR WEEK

Monday	$105.70
Tuesday	96.94
Wednesday	127.35
Thursday	93.15
Friday	101.72
Total	$524.86

efficiency of the servers. Therefore, we will just say that one without the others is much like a three-legged stool.

Serving Schedule for the Line

Managers should post serving schedules to save time, questions, and confusion.

Serving schedules should include all of the information listed below.

1. Who will be responsible for setting up the line. (This could include, for example, preheating of the wells in the serving counter with dry or moist heat or taking the initial pans of food and serving utensils to the line.)

2. Who will serve in each position
3. Who will clean the serving counter
4. Who will put food away
5. Who will count the milk and clean the milk box
6. Who will be the designated runner (the person who keeps the food supply replenished for the serving counter). This person may also be assigned to keep up with the cook-as-served items, such as french fries.

The persons who are serving should never leave the serving counter while customers are coming through the line. Servers must be (1) calm and friendly and portray a we-care-about-you image; (2) coordinated and able to use both hands for serving; and (3) able to serve rapidly and keep the serving counter neat.

We do not recommend that assistants who are assigned to the serving line rotate responsibilities, but if managers feel that they must rotate employees on the serving line with employees having other responsibilities, employees must meet the above criteria and the rotation should occur no more than once each month.

Serving Schedule for the Dishroom

The serving schedule for the dishroom should include all of the information listed below.

1. Who will fill the dish machine and what time it should be filled
2. Who will keep the dish machine filled with soap
3. Who will check the water temperatures of the wash cycle and the rinse cycle
4. Who will work the dish-return window. (Note: This employee needs a good disposition and must be coordinated.)
5. Who will work the clean end of the dish machine
6. Who will return eating utensils and trays to the serving counter
7. Who will store permanent ware
8. Who will clean the drain baskets or strainers in the dish machine

9. Who will clean the dish machine thoroughly
10. Who will keep the dish carts clean
11. Who will bleach dish trays

The after-serving schedule should contain the following information:

1. Who will wash pots and pans
2. Who will do general cleanup or "clutter cleaning"
3. Who will clean the tables and chairs in the dining room
4. Who will do special assignments

Cleanup Schedule

"Everybody's business is nobody's business" is a saying that applies to cleaning the kitchen and the equipment. A manager has the ultimate responsibility for keeping the kitchen sparkling clean so that germ and bacteria growth cannot occur. Rodents and bugs will take up residence elsewhere. And justifiable pride can come with the image created.

In order to make "everybody's business everybody's business," a manager must assign all cleanup responsibilities *in writing* to a specific person or persons. (Cleanup responsibilities may be assigned on the production schedule to employees who do not have heavy production assignments on a specific day.) It is also the manager's responsibility to follow up with employees to make sure that each area is indeed cleaned thoroughly.

The manager should post the cleanup record, and as assistants clean the assigned area, they should date and initial the activity in the appropriate column after the activity is completed. See the sample that follows.

> ***Did you ever notice that last night's TV miniseries generates more discussion in the kitchen than the last six in-service meetings?***

Sample Cleanup Schedule

	Sept.	Oct.	Nov.	Dec.	Jan.	Feb.	March	April	May	June
Steamer ☐ Blow down ☐ Clean drains ☐ Remove racks & clean ☐ Remove door panels & clean ☐ Wash outside incl. legs ☐ Other _____										
Steam Kettle ☐ Clean outside bottom of kettle ☐ Drain (clean daily) ☐ Cabinet, incl. legs ☐ Clean lid (both sides)										
Ovens ☐ Remove racks and wash ☐ Clean inside w/oven cleaner. (*Do not* leave oven cleaner on overnight. *Do not* use oven cleaner on self-cleaning ovens.) ☐ Remove and clean oven fan guard ☐ Clean glass on doors ☐ Wash outside incl. legs ☐ Clean gaskets										

Sample Cleanup Schedule (continued)

	Sept.	Oct.	Nov.	Dec.	Jan.	Feb.	March	April	May	June
Stove ☐ Wash outside incl. legs ☐ Clean oven if applicable										
Work and Bake Tables ☐ Wash tops, under shelves, & drawers ☐ Clean drawers ☐ Organize utensils in drawer ☐ Wash outside of bins (if applicable)										
Pass-throughs ☐ Remove pan racks ☐ Wash inside incl. floor. (Do not leave crumbs from one day until the next.)										
Pan Racks ☐ Remove pans ☐ Wash thoroughly incl. posts and slides										
Bun Warmer/Proof Cabinet ☐ Wash inside (incl. tray slides) ☐ Wash outside. (*Do not allow grease buildup. Do not leave crumbs.*)										

Reach-in Refrigerator/Freezer ☐ Remove racks and wash in warm soda water ☐ Clean inside w/warm soda water ☐ Remove any spoiled or old food ☐ Clean up spills ☐ Clean gaskets ☐ Wash outside incl. legs							
Walk-in Refrigerator/Freezer ☐ Organize stock ☐ Sweep ☐ Clean shelves & dollies ☐ Clean up spills ☐ Mop floor ☐ Remove any spoiled food							
Sinks (Pot & Pan, Vegetable) ☐ Wash outside incl. legs							
Lavatories in Kitchen ☐ Clean with cleanser							
Bathroom ☐ Clean fixtures w/disinfectant ☐ Empty trash cans ☐ Replenish paper towels & soap ☐ Sweep & hose floor							
Vent Hoods ☐ Wash outside ☐ Wash inside ☐ Remove filters & run through dish machine							

Staffing Formulas and Patterns

The scheduling of staff in order to make maximum use of each employee's time and talents is critical to having an efficient, effective foodservice program. A manager needs to decide on the best staffing patterns within the staffing formula or productivity standard provided. The staffing formula or productivity standard is the total number of hours needed to serve a specific number of meals. The staffing formula or productivity standard below is based on a majority of the menu items being prepared from scratch, with the exception of the foods for à la carte, short-order, or sandwich lines. Managers can adjust Meals Per Labor Hour (MPLH) according to their own operations.

Staffing Formula

Productivity Standard	Average # Meals
15–18 MPLH	High schools with short order
15 MPLH	500 and above
14 MPLH	375–499
13 MPLH	300–374
12 MPLH	250–299
11 MPLH	225–249
10 MPLH	200–224
9 MPLH	150–199

To calculate the number of hours of labor needed, divide the average number of meals by the productivity standard. Example: If a school is serving 450 meals a day, the manager would need thirty-two hours of labor. The more convenience foods that managers use, the fewer labor hours they should use.

Using the example of a school serving 450 meals and having thirty-two labor hours, managers may develop a staffing pattern similar to one of those that follow.

Did you ever notice that, while a watched pot never boils, an unwatched pot always boils . . . over?

Sample Staffing Patterns

Manager	7.5 hours
2 employees @ 5.5 hours	11.0 hours
1 employee @ 5 hours	5.0 hours
1 employee @ 4½ hours	4.5 hours
1 employee @ 2 hours	2.0 hours
1 cashier @ 2 hours	2.0 hours
	32.0 hours
Manager	7.5 hours
3 employees @ 5 hours	15.0 hours
1 employee @ 4½ hours	4.5 hours
1 employee @ 3 hours	3.0 hours
1 employee @ 2 hours	2.0 hours
	32.0 hours
Manager	7.5 hours
1 employee @ 5½ hours	5.5 hours
2 employees @ 5 hours	10.0 hours
1 employee @ 4 hours	4.0 hours
1 employee @ 3 hours	3.0 hours
1 employee @ 2 hours	2.0 hours
	32.0 hours

If the maximum number of hours is not used daily, the manager may choose to ask the staff (or the person(s) assigned to prepare a specific menu item) to come in earlier on days when the preparation is more difficult, such as with school-made pizza or fried chicken. If a school is expecting a large number of guests on any given day, the manager should make arrangements for additional labor. If more than thirty guests are expected, a rule of thumb is to allow one hour for each additional fifteen meals prepared and served.

The success of a foodservice program depends on the efficiency and speed of the staff when meals are served to customers. Competent managers determine the number of employees needed during the serving period(s) and begin the staffing pattern with that number

Did you ever notice that just about the time that you feel you can take a break, something else does?

of employees. For example, a manager in a school serving 450 lunches with one serving line may decide that he or she needs the following employees at serving time.

2	people serving
1	cashier
1	backup person (or runner)
2	employees in the dishroom
6	employees needed at serving time

If there is a break between classes coming through the line, one person from the serving line can take the trays from the racks and stack them during the break while other assistants replenish the food and clean up any spills. The cashier can roll money, straighten the milk in the milk box, and check the dispensers.

School foodservice managers have long ceased to be "little old ladies in tennis shoes." The competency of their management can be measured by (1) the number of satisfied customers who return day after day for good-tasting food; (2) the quality and variety of that food, prepared from the best ingredients and served in an attractive and efficient manner; and (3) the efficiency of the total operation, particularly with regard to the time and talents of the professionals who make that operation run smoothly.

The majority of managers have those management competencies and are successful. However, the word *successful* is relative. No program is the perfect one—*yet*.

We are counting on *you* for the *yet*!

Did you ever notice that the day that the dough doesn't rise is the day that the PTA president is coming to lunch?

The Casserole Caper (Part 1)

It never fails, thought Jessie as she hurried to answer her jangling phone. Just when the serving line begins to bunch up and every hand is needed to unclog it, someone decides that that's the only time to call. "Mrs. Pritchard," she said into the phone. She pressed a finger into her left ear to cut out the noise of fifty kids all talking at the same time as they passed down the serving line.

"Good morning, Miss Jessie, and how are you this morning? I hope I caught you at a good time."

Jessie shook her head and closed her eyes as she listened to the all-too-familiar voice of Evelyn Stutz. She was the PTA president this year, and she took her job very seriously—too seriously. Nothing that happened at the school or within a ten-mile radius of it was beyond Mrs. Stutz's involvement. Or perhaps *interference* was a better word.

Jessie had always prided herself on building and keeping good relations with the PTA. They could be and were valuable supporters not only of the school but also of the food-service program. Whenever there was a PTA board meeting, Jessie made sure that the school's activity fund could cover refreshments that produced exclamations from dieters and

89

nondieters alike. And most years the appreciation was returned. Most PTA presidents and board members were grateful that they had not had to whip up desserts themselves those nights before their meetings. But not Evelyn Stutz. She was that rare exception—the thoroughly obnoxious person who knew everything about everything and at the drop of a syllable would proceed to tell you more than you really wanted to know.

"So I was wondering when I could come over and talk to you about it," Mrs. Stutz was saying.

Jessie held the phone away for a second and stared at it. *Talk about what?* She quickly recovered. "There is so much noise here that I didn't quite catch all that you said."

"Oh, never mind, dear," Evelyn Stutz said without much conviction, "I'll see you at two o'clock and explain in detail what I have in mind. Okay?"

"You mean today?" Jessie asked. There was no reply. The phone was dead. Jessie seldom swore, but this was one of those times. She was muttering to herself when she returned to check the serving line.

Mary Lou kept both hands going as she looked up and saw Jessie's expression. "You didn't win the Irish Sweepstakes, right?"

Jessie smiled in spite of herself. "Hardly. I've got an appointment at two with someone I don't particularly care for to talk about I-don't-know-what. And besides that, she called me 'dear.'"

Mary Lou stifled a giggle. "Oh dear."

"All right, all right," Jessie laughed, "I imagine I'll survive. Now, what do we need up here? I'd better see about some more rolls."

At two o'clock Jessie was bent over the day's production schedule and didn't hear the footsteps that stopped at the cafeteria door.

"Hello," called a too-cheerful voice, "anybody home?"

Jessie's head jerked up and turned to the doorway. Evelyn Stutz walked into the kitchen. "There you are," she chirped.

Isn't she the clever one, Jessie thought, and she tried to unclench her teeth. Jessie stood and extended her hand. "Hello, Mrs. Stutz. Let me pull up a chair. And could I get you some tea or coffee?"

"No thank you, dear." *There was that "dear" again,* thought Jessie. "And please call me Evelyn. Now, about my idea, Miss Jessie. I thought. . . ."

"Yes, about your idea, Mrs . . . er . . . Evelyn. Why don't you start at the beginning," Jessie said with a straight face. She didn't have the slightest idea of what might be coming.

Evelyn Stutz looked puzzled, but only for an instant. "Well, as I said on the phone, Tommy . . . you know my boy, Tommy?"

Jessie nodded and smiled. *How a good kid like that could have. . . .*

"Tommy," Evelyn Stutz ran on, "doesn't say much about school unless his father and I drag it out of him."

I'll just bet he doesn't say much. How could he, thought Jessie. Then she checked herself. *Pay attention,* she told herself. *We may finally be getting to the point.*

"Anyway," Mrs. Stutz continued, "I asked Tommy about your menus here, and he gave me a general idea of what you serve our children. Now, I don't have any criticism. Not at all. You do a marvelous job. And all of us are very grateful for what you're doing. But . . ."

Here it comes, Jessie thought, as she held a half smile in place.

"Some of us . . ."

Jessie interrupted. "Some of us, Mrs. Stutz? Now how many would that be?"

"Well, I don't exactly remember, but that's really not important. I'll come right to the point, Miss Jessie. We think that you should experiment with some new recipes."

Evelyn Stutz waited for a response from Jessie. Jessie just smiled and nodded slightly. The silence lengthened.

Mrs. Stutz could not abide silence. She rattled on. "Now, what I was thinking is that from what Tommy has told me you don't have a lot of variety in your menus. Now, I know that you have the Youth Advisory Council to try new menu items with, but what I'm thinking about is . . ."

Here it comes, Jessie thought. *Finally.*

"Surprising the kids with a new casserole that I know of. A very good one that just everybody loves," Evelyn concluded and waited for a response once again. None came. Jessie smiled and waited.

Embarrassed, Evelyn continued. "Now, I know what you're thinking. That I'm just a crazy mother . . ."

Jessie's expression didn't flicker.

". . . who is trying to butt in where she doesn't belong. But I'm just trying to help the school and you all. Mrs. Stevens at the nursing home tried it and even translated my recipe into large-quantity size. I watched the preparation very carefully. So . . . so what do you think, Miss Jessie? When would you like to try it?"

Jessie didn't answer immediately. Evelyn Stutz fidgeted in her chair. "Mrs. Stutz, I am somewhat surprised at your interest in our foodservice program. But pleased. I do have a couple of questions, though."

"Certainly," Mrs. Stutz beamed.

"Did Mrs. Stevens do a portion cost analysis for your casserole?" Jessie asked.

"Well, not exactly."

"And what kind of reception did your casserole have at the nursing home?"

Evelyn Stutz answered without hesitation. "Oh, they just loved it. I know. It was my secret ingredient!"

"Oh, did you check for any plate waste after the meal?" Jessie queried. "And what is your secret ingredient?"

"Plate waste? Plate waste? Why on earth should there have been any plate waste? It's a perfectly marvelous recipe," Mrs. Stutz concluded lamely.

"I see," Jessie answered. Then she continued. "I'll tell you what. Since you know your recipe better than anyone and since I know you want to make sure that it's done right, when would you be free to come in and help us prepare it? Oh, and do plan to stay long enough to see how much the students enjoy your casserole."

"Well, I really hadn't planned . . . ," Evelyn Stutz started.

She didn't get any further. Jessie interrupted. "Oh, but you must help us. It will be a special treat, I know. And your fine hand would just have to be there. Now, let me see," Jessie said as she looked over her production schedule. "Let's say Friday the fourteenth. And between now and, let's say, next Tuesday, you can get me the recipe so that I can order the food that we'll need."

Jessie stood and held out her hand. "So . . . I'll be looking for that recipe. And do hold open the fourteenth. Shall we say eight o'clock that morning?"

"Well, I . . . ," Mrs. Stutz sputtered.

"We'll be delighted to see you." Jessie moved toward the cafeteria. Evelyn Stutz rose and followed. Jessie stood aside for her to pass. "Oh, and Mrs. Stutz, would you do me a favor?"

Evelyn Stutz was in mild shock. How had she gotten into this? She nodded and muttered something.

"I'll invite the rest of the PTA board for lunch. I would really appreciate your calling them on the thirteenth to remind them," Jessie said, with the kind of smile lost on Evelyn Stutz.

"But . . . but, I really don't think . . ."

Jessie smiled broadly and pretended not to hear. "We'll look forward to getting your recipe Tuesday. I'll call you Tuesday afternoon, and we'll see you early Friday morning."

Jessie waved, turned, and walked quickly back to her desk. She didn't see a grim-faced Evelyn Stutz raise her hand, start to speak, change her mind, and walk from the cafeteria. She was shaking her head.

But, then, so was Jessie.

What's for Lunch?

Managers can have the best staff, the best supervisory skills, and the best work schedules; but if they don't have another "best" to go with those, they might as well hang up their hairnets. That other "best" is *menus*.

Competent managers know that a primary management focus must be on the best menus that they can plan, prepare, and present to their customers. And if managers sometimes feel that customers do not always know best, they also know that without them, foodservice programs cease to operate.

Much like a juggler with five balls in the air at the same time, school foodservice managers must be aware constantly of the *acceptability* of their menus to customers; the *nutritional value* of menu components; the cost of the *labor* it takes to prepare, serve, and clean up after meals; the *cost and quality* of food used in preparation; and those ever-present *"other" costs* that are too often glossed over.

Managers decide the acceptability of their menus by

- Planning and preparing attractive foods and menus that customers enjoy
- Making each menu item look so attractive and inviting that customers cannot resist selecting it
- Serving food in an attractive atmosphere
- Serving a large variety of foods seasoned "just right"
- Involving customers in menu decision-making

Managers determine the nutritional value of foodservice programs by

- Planning meals that meet specified meal patterns
- Cooking, storing, and serving foods with care to preserve nutrients
- Eliminating excessive sugar, salt, and fats from the menus

Managers control the cost of menus as well as "other" costs by

- Using the minimum number of labor hours needed to produce quality products
- Keeping a close watch on portion sizes
- Evaluating each food product based on its value to the program
- Meeting the meal pattern requirements first, and adding "something extra" only when additional calories are needed and if there is money available
- Comparing prices on similar items from at least two companies
- Checking merchandise to be sure that the product delivered was the product purchased
- Watching market conditions and serving foods that are in plentiful supply
- Judging products by the customers' standards
- Using the "right product" for the "right job"
- Keeping an accurate record of the quantity of foods used
- Keeping a record of the number of meals and number or quantity of menu items served daily
- Basing projected quantities of food to be prepared on previous menu items served daily
- Preparing food as close to serving time as possible
- Planning and preparing the correct amount of food—not too much and not too little
- Avoiding overproduction by implementing a "¼, ½, ¾ checkpoint" system. (When ¼ of the students have gone through the

line, check to see whether ¼ of each menu item has been served.)

- Purchasing *only* products needed to maintain or improve the program
- Monitoring the quantities of detergent, cleaning, and other consumable supplies used and calculating the "real" cost per day or cost per meal
- Adopting a "no waste, no abuse" policy for items such as garbage bags and aluminum foil

Managers can manage a menu only when they recognize good menus and evaluate them regularly by the customers' reactions. A good menu

- Invites customers with colors, textures, flavors, shapes, and combinations
- Is cooked "just right" and seasoned to perfection
- Is one that customers enjoy eating
- Meets the food needs (meal pattern) of the customers
- Satisfies hungry appetites
- Is served rapidly and attractively
- Is produced and served within budget (including labor limitations)
- Is served with a good attitude, great pride, and a smile

When food looks attractive and smells inviting, the customer will taste it. When the food pleases the palate, the customer will eat it. When customers enjoy the food and feel they are getting good value for their money, they will become repeat customers and bring their friends with them.

The quality of a menu or the items on that menu cannot be guaranteed by reading words or completing checklists. However, a menu checklist, such as the following sample, can remind managers of the key things to look for every time a menu is planned and served. Adapt the sample to your own program and keep it within easy reach.

We cannot give you a surefire menu plan that will fit *your* customers'

Sample Menu Checklist

	Mon.	Tues.	Weds.	Thurs.	Fri.
Does the menu contain					
Foods that will invite customers to eat?					
A choice of menu items?					
A 2 oz. serving of meat/meat alternate in one or two menu items?					
A good natural source of vitamin C?					
A good source of vitamin A?					
One or more servings of bread?					
Several different shapes of menu items?					
A pretty color scheme?					
How many menu items does each menu contain?					
Something crisp?					
Something soft?					
A "spicy taste"?					
A mild or bland taste?					
Will the menu satisfy a hungry customer?					

needs. There are just too many different factors that determine what customers like to eat. Spicy foods will be very popular in one part of the country and avoided like the plague in another. Customers in East Normal like gravy over anything except lemon meringue pie. Those in West Nowhere will scrape it off, convinced that you are trying to hide a mistake.

    Competent managers waste no time in finding out what foods appeal most to their customers. They watch carefully to see which menu items "sell." They make it a point to be at the tray-return window when a breakfast or lunch period is over. They will determine what food was not eaten and whether there was a pattern to the amount or types of food wasted.

    When in doubt, ask your customers what was good and not so good—and why. Work with your principal and faculty to conduct a "food favorites" survey among students, or ask the Student Council to get homeroom reaction to your menus, or ask a popular teacher to plan a menu for a day (with your help!), or ask Ms. Smith's fifth-grade class to plan their favorite menu.

The line is straight and short between a cost-effective school meal that also reflects customers' food preferences. But—a word of caution—school foodservices are nutrition programs. Our goal is to meet one-third of the nutritional requirements or food needs of the young people we serve. Plan menus carefully, and be cautious with sugar, salt, and the starches. Serve no more than a bread and one menu item with a high starch content (rice, macaroni, spaghetti, potatoes, corn, dry beans or peas, puddings, cakes, and so forth).

When students are helping to plan menus and suggest two or more menu items with high starch content, managers have an opportunity to teach nutrition education by pointing out the reasons that they should select another food to replace one of the starchy menu items. It is also possible to offer the two "starch" items as a choice—and allow them to select one.

U.S. Department of Agriculture Commodities

USDA commodities are vital to the successful operation of school foodservice programs. Of generally high quality, these foods can make the difference between a financially sound program and a losing one.

Because commodities are received at little or no expense to foodservice programs, they are viewed by some as "free," and therefore without monetary value. Nothing could be further from the truth. Competent managers are well aware that without the grain, meat, fruit, vegetable, and other commodity products, their purchased food costs would soar. It is the wise manager, therefore, who treats either processed or raw commodities as money in the foodservice account. And equally wise are those managers who impress this fact upon their assistants.

- Do not attempt to stockpile commodities in order to "save" them. You may end up with some that you cannot use, but equally important is the fact that your "hoarding" may be depriving another school's child of the best meal he or she can have.

- Make sure that you follow the "first in, first out" rule. And this applies not only to commodities, but also to all stored food. Make sure that you date every delivered item and use first those foods that you received first. A sound inventory system is one of the best friends of a competent manager.

- If you prepare food from scratch, keep an eye out for new recipes that make use of commodities and that will appeal to your customers. Not only will you add variety to your choices, but you also will be able to build that most important part of every school foodservice program—student participation.

Purchasing Procedures

For most school foodservice programs, labor leads the "cost" list. Not far behind are the costs of food and necessary supplies. Just as good scheduling and supervision make the most of foodservice talent, wise purchasing procedures make the most of every food/supplies dollar.

Purchasing procedures vary a great deal from one school district to another. Many districts have bid and specification rules that are very rigid. Others allow some degree of flexibility when it comes to purchasing needed food and supplies. Regardless of the procedures used, managers must make hard-nosed business decisions—often. The most competent managers have specific guidelines that they follow. Below are a few, but certainly not all of them.

- Good quality does not always wear a high-priced label. Whether your district uses a bid system or not, everything is determined by the standards *you* set for *your* customers' food needs. If you feel that you have no control over what your district allows you to buy, you might be pleasantly surprised at the response when you can tell *exactly* why brand X will not meet your needs and *exactly* why brand Y will.

- If your school district uses a bid system, make sure that you purchase all items from the bid lists.

- Purchase products at the lowest price *unless* you have a specific reason to justify buying the product at a higher price.

- Document the prices quoted to you for comparison on your production records. You never know when you may need justification.

- Compare products received (weight, quantity, and quality) with the specifications on your order.

- Evaluate and select each product based on its value and/or contribution to the school foodservice program.

- Purchase foods to meet the meal pattern *first,* and, if there is money left, you may purchase extra-calorie foods ("something extra").

- Evaluate prepared food carefully. The prices of prepared or convenience foods have the cost of labor built in. Can you afford to pay labor twice? Compare the cost per serving of prepared or convenience foods with your products made from scratch. To get a true comparison, include the cost of the labor required to make the product from scratch. Compare the quality of prepared or convenience foods with products made from scratch. Are the prepared or convenience foods as acceptable to your customers as the ones made from scratch?

Competent managers know that it takes supplies other than food to run a school foodservice program well. Chemicals, for example, are a major supply need. When you have that need, consider the recommendations below.

- Buy chemicals very carefully and for specific needs *only.*

- Compare prices from two or three companies.

- Avoid large investments of money.

- Buy *only* quantities that can be used in a reasonable period of time, like three months.

- Avoid "pressure" salesmen who *must take* the order on the day of the visit.

Below are some questions you need to ask yourself when you are ready to purchase chemicals.

- What is the *total cost* of the product?

- Does this price include freight and/or delivery costs?
- How will the product benefit my program?
- Will the overall effectiveness of my program be damaged if I do not buy the product?
- Is the product really worth the money?
- Can I "think about" the product for a day or two and then order it? (Time often helps us "sort out" the need for the product versus the total cost.)
- What other schools nearby are using the product? (Call those managers and ask if the product is as good as claimed and if the price is reasonable.)

Computers

A good manager would be lost if there were no oven handy when it came time to bake rolls. A lump of dough on a serving-line plate would not interest too many customers. That oven is the most important tool for the manager at baking time, and the same thing can be said at other times about other pieces of equipment that make a school kitchen operate efficiently.

A tool that is becoming increasingly important to managers, even though it causes some to shudder at the thought, is the computer. The idea of sitting down in front of a computer is as threatening to some people as the idea of taking the controls of a 747 landing at O'Hare Airport. But just as it was frightening the first time someone put dough into a hot oven, a first experience with a computer may be terrifying, but it need not be.

It helps a great deal to put it all in perspective. Every day, you and your assistants generate a whole raft of information that tells you what

Did you ever notice that some reporting forms make a lot more sense when you read them upside down?

it costs to prepare the meal you served and how much income was realized as a result of your efforts. If you are like most managers, you have recorded that information for reporting purposes on a daily, weekly, or monthly basis. You probably do the recording on paper, and sometime later you compile each day's records, then add, subtract, divide, and multiply to come up with the monthly report that is required by your school, school district, and state Department of Education. You could save hours of time, grief, and aggravation with all of those figures on paper if you used a computer.

In the last few years, major breakthroughs in the cost and design of computers, particularly personal ones, have come about. Most manufacturers recognize that a key selling point is that their computers must be "user-friendly." That means simply that it does not take a genius to learn to operate one. In fact, using one can be downright fun.

For some time, many foodservice professionals refused to become involved with computers because of a lack of software, but now there are approximately 150 software packages designed specifically for school foodservice use.

If your foodservice operation serves more than 500 customers a day, a twenty-quart mixer will never meet all of your needs. The same comparison applies to computers. If you think you are ready to take advantage of the benefits and services that a computer can provide, and if the choice is up to you, you will need to inventory your particular situation first.

Many foodservice managers are employed in large school districts that have large main-frame computers and use local school terminals to receive and send data. Even in these situations, managers need to be aware of what computers can do for them. And, when the time comes, it is important to know enough about computers to speak up about what services a computerized accounting system can provide.

If your foodservice operation is of the size and readiness to look into the many time-saving advantages that a computer can provide, there are some basic questions that need to be asked and that only you can answer.

- Are you satisfied with the way that you now record your costs, income/inventory, and menu plans? How much time does it take?

- What information could you use that you do not have now that would simplify your job and improve your foodservice program?
- Do you have the money to buy the hardware (the computer itself) and the software that you need, *and* can you show how much money could be saved through better recordkeeping?
- Do you have the support of your supervisor for getting and using a computer?
- Is there someone in your district who knows about computers that you can turn to for help when you need to?
- Are you willing to take the time to learn to use a computer and to teach someone on your staff to use it as well?

Good News and Bad News About Computers

The good news is that real cost savings can be realized with computer use. A computer offers the potential for cutting food costs, for scheduling labor hours more efficiently, for maintaining smaller inventories of purchased food, and for keeping better track of both direct and indirect costs. And not only will savings be realized, but you can keep a day-by-day running tally of your costs and income, instead of waiting until the end of the month to see how you managed.

More good news. You will have the ability to spot problem areas early—problems such as purchased-food costs and decreases in participation. If you want to tie your food usage to your ordering procedure, the opportunity also is there. You can also store menus and standard recipes on a computer. Some school districts record their free/reduced student participation data on a computer, as well as student survey results.

The bad news? First of all, changing over to a computerized system takes time. You will need time to set up the system and then time to debug it. (More about that below.) If you are short on patience and have trouble envisioning long-term benefits, tread carefully.

While computers and software have become much less expensive than they were even a few years ago, a major investment of time and money will be necessary. Do not make that investment until you know exactly what you want the computer to do. It is just as easy to overbuy equipment that you do not need as it is to underbuy equipment that lacks the capacity to handle your requirements.

Then there is the matter of people and how they react to change. Some can roll with the punches. Some cannot. It may be necessary for you to sell the *idea* of using a computer before you have the equipment on hand. Along with introducing the idea, sell the benefits that each person will gain by using the computer. In the final analysis, each person has to "buy in."

And one more word of caution. Do not throw out the recordkeeping system you are using until your computer program has been running successfully for anywhere from six months to a year, to back up your computer program.

Because school foodservice operations vary so much from one school to another and from one district to another, it is nearly impossible to prescribe exactly which computer system would be best. Regardless of operational size, however, there are some basic pieces of advice that apply to anyone moving to a computerized recordkeeping system.

- Know your foodservice operation well enough so that you can explain every detail of it to a computer programmer or software salesperson.

- Be able to identify *in priority order* what you want the computer to do for you. In other words, what is the most important recordkeeping or production job that you have to do that the computer could help you with? The next most important? And the next?

- Prepare to spend some time scrutinizing software packages in light of the priorities that you have identified. Ask *plenty* of questions. One of the first mistakes that a person can make when computer shopping is to take a sales pitch at face value or a nod as full understanding of your needs.

- Whether you are buying a foodservice software package or are involved in designing a program from scratch, the first steps are critical so that you start up with as few "bugs" as possible. (Bugs are gaps or mistakes or glitches that you did not plan for but that can stop you cold.) The early stage—the startup—requires more of that precious commodity: time. Design of a program or inputting information into an existing package is a slow, step-by-step process. Test your steps as you go—and go slowly. Care and thoroughness will pay off in the long run—and the short run, too.

- If you have a say in choosing the computer hardward itself, keep in mind what you have heard many times—KISS! (Keep It Simple, Stupid.) Keep the user-friendly idea right up front. Think of the people with whom you work who may use the equipment. Think of how you might train people on that computer. Of course it is essential that you feel comfortable with it, but will others with whom you work feel comfortable with the equipment you choose?

- You will notice that we have placed a lot of emphasis on choosing the right software for your computer. That emphasis is intentional. One of the greatest mistakes that anyone can make is to buy a computer because it is a bargain and then to try to fit a software program to it. In many cases, this is square-peg-in-round-hole time. Know what you want a computer to do for you (your priorities), choose the software package that will do the job for you, and then search out the computer that is flexible enough to handle your program now *and* later.

- Just as you plan a menu and the production schedule to go with it, plan your computer project in the same way. Think ahead. Plan your steps carefully, one at a time. And put those steps in a time frame. The whens are just as important as the whats and the hows. Your time frame will almost certainly change, but you will need some benchmarks to work from. Be flexible but be consistent. It will pay off in the end.

- As you move into the computer world, you will hear a great deal about program bugs. No computer program is perfect, so plan for how you will handle debugging. Just as you have a pest-control program for your cafeteria, make sure that you have a debugging control built into your computer efforts. And that means that there should be someone whom you can call on for help. The person needs to be someone who knows your foodservice operation and who has been kept up to date on your progress with computerization. Whether this person is a school-district programmer or your software salesperson or a willing and knowledgeable friend, stick to him or her like glue until your computer operation is up and running successfully.

If all of this sounds too complicated to touch with a ten-foot pole, it is not meant to be so. It is just that to accomplish anything worthwhile requires work. A growing number of foodservice managers have found that computers are definitely worthwhile—for greater accountability, for eliminating paperwork, and, most important, for making better use of time, your most important resource. The computer is the most exciting and useful tool to become available to the foodservice manager since fire was invented!

Did you ever notice that just about the time you have found the one recipe for commodity prunes that kids like, you are no longer getting any?

The Casserole Caper (Part 2)

For the sixth or seventh time, Jessie looked at the recipe in front of her. *She can't be serious,* Jessie thought. *Does Evelyn Stutz really think that a glorified tuna casserole is going to create a student stampede to the serving line? And that secret ingredient—slivered water chestnuts! You'd better believe they'll be slivered,* Jessie mused. She had done a cost analysis, and with 100 servings, they could more than break even. The recipe was for 200 servings, but Jessie knew her students well enough to know that even 100 could be too many.

It was 7:45, and in a few minutes Evelyn Stutz would come sweeping through the door, ready to show them how to operate a school foodservice program.

"Mary Lou," Jessie called as she stood up from her desk and went into the kitchen. She saw Mary Lou checking the casserole ingredients laid out on one end of the preparation table. Mary Lou turned and smiled. "It's all here and waiting, Jessie," Mary Lou said, and paused. "Just how much time do you want me to spend with her putting this thing together?"

"We'll follow the production schedule just like we always

do," Jessie answered. "But keep one eye on the clock and another on how Mrs. Stutz is coming along. Chances are that it's going to be nip and tuck as to which is finished first—the lunch periods or her casserole."

"Jessie," Mary Lou asked, "isn't it kind of unusual to have a parent helping to cook lunch?"

Jessie smiled and nodded. "Unusual? Yes. Necessary? Definitely. We've needed a way for a long time to let people know that preparing a meal every day for a thousand kids is not exactly a cakewalk. And what better way to get our point across than with the PTA president? I have a feeling that before the sun goes down, half the town will get a full account of what happened here today."

Mary Lou didn't answer.

"You think I'm a darned fool," Jessie asked, "taking a chance like this?"

"Well . . . ," Mary Lou began.

"You're absolutely right!" Jessie interrupted, grinning. "But I have a couple of aces up my sleeve." She winked and turned as the back door slammed

Evelyn Stutz was quite a sight. She was wearing a white uniform that was at least two sizes too small and a pair of white sneakers that looked two sizes too large. Her hair was straight, struggling to escape from a hairnet that had seen better days. From her ears dangled large loops of gold. She was wearing black eye liner—far too much of it. Jessie's first thought was that she looked like a raccoon dressed as Minnie Mouse.

"I couldn't find a thing to wear but my old nurse's uniform, but it still fits pretty well, don't you think?" Evelyn Stutz asked as she put her hands on her more-than-ample hips.

The ringing of the phone saved Jessie and Mary Lou from having to answer her.

"Excuse me just a second," Jessie muttered as she moved to her desk. Mary Lou would have to handle that one alone.

Jessie picked up the phone. Ginger was crying into it. She was near the babbling stage. A "perfectly horrid" man had run into her car on the way to work. She wasn't hurt, but both cars were pretty badly damaged and the other driver was blaming her and the police weren't there yet and she didn't know what to do and . . .

Jessie kept the phone to her ear, making soothing sounds, but her mind was on the fact that she was going to be short two hands with a potential catastrophe in the kitchen.

"Well, honey, just sort it out as best you can, and come on in if at all possible. You'll see. It will all work out," Jessie said calmly. She didn't feel as calm as she tried to sound.

"Oh, I'll be in." Ginger sounded more like herself now that the shock was wearing off and she'd heard a friendly voice. "I just don't know how long it'll be, Jessie."

"I know, Ginger, I know," Jessie answered. "See you soon."

Jessie hung up and looked at the clock. Five minutes past eight. *I could try for a sub,* she thought. But she knew she wouldn't be able to get one for at least an hour, and by that time . . . Jessie smiled to herself and nodded.

"Evelyn," Jessie said as she returned to the kitchen, "that was one of my assistants. She's had an accident on the way to school. She's not hurt, but she will be delayed. How would you like to be a real member of the team?"

"But what about my casserole? I see that all the things I need are . . . ," Evelyn began.

"Oh, don't worry, we'll have the casserole. But we may need some extra hands." And they did.

By 10:30 Evelyn Stutz looked as though she had been pulled through a knothole backward. Her hairnet had given up, and she periodically had to blow strands of hair out of her eyes. She had a black streak extending from her left eyelid to her left ear, where she had absentmindedly wiped away some perspiration. But she stuck it out. Periodically, Jessie had suggested that she take a break, since she wasn't used to the pace. Evelyn had shaken her head and doggedly worked on her casserole while lending a hand to half a dozen other tasks.

At 10:45 Ginger walked in the back door, filled with righteous indignation against "that twit" whose car had rear-ended hers. Jessie let her know that the report would have to wait. The kids would be arriving in twenty minutes.

"Twenty minutes?" Evelyn Stutz shrieked. "My casserole will never be ready in twenty minutes. The cheese isn't brown yet. It isn't bubbling yet."

Jessie strode over and peeked into the oven. "Turn it up forty degrees and watch it carefully, Evelyn. When that bell rings, we serve."

And they did. Everything. Except for thirty-five servings of tuna casserole. Four members of the PTA board selected it. When they returned their trays to the dish-return window, Jessie and Evelyn were there checking trays. Jessie almost felt guilty. Almost. She felt as though she were rubbing Evelyn's face in her own tuna casserole. The board members made clucking sounds of approval over the casserole. The kids didn't. Most of what went out from the line came back to the dish-return window.

It was a dejected and haggard Evelyn Stutz who slumped into a chair at the staff's dining table, gulping her second glass of iced tea.

"I don't remember the last time I was this tired. The only things that don't hurt are my earlobes, and that's only because I took off those stupid earrings when one almost got caught in the can opener," she mumbled to no one in particular.

"Yes, there are days like that," Jessie commiserated.

"But you do this every day. And how you do it, I don't know," Evelyn said, looking at Jessie.

"We learn how to take the fewest steps between the most jobs, Evelyn. Let me say that I admire you for coming in here and accomplishing what you did today."

"Accomplishing, my foot! I had to be shown how to do every job—sometimes twice. And as for my casserole idea, the less said the better."

"Don't be so hard on yourself. Next time . . . ," Jessie got no further.

"Next time? Next time?" Evelyn almost shouted. "Believe me, there will be no next time. I learned a valuable lesson today. I wouldn't have gone into a classroom and tried to teach algebra. I wouldn't have tried to coach football. What made me think I could do quantity cooking?"

There was dead silence. Slowly, Evelyn Stutz raised her head and stared at Jessie. Then a smile began to part her lips. "Miss Jessie, you're something else. You knew how this would turn out all along, didn't you? Now, didn't you?" Evelyn's smile turned to a chuckle.

Jessie looked at her closely and saw that, where a week before she had had an adversary, she now had a friend. And then Jessie laughed too. "I didn't know, Evelyn. I really didn't know how it would turn out. If I'd said 'no,' it wouldn't have been fair to you and I would likely have made an enemy. I figured that if I said 'yes,' I had nothing to lose and a lot to gain. I think that maybe we both gained something."

They had. And for years afterward, when they'd meet, sometimes they would laugh and exchange recipes for casseroles.

Managing Nagging Problems

Change. Stress. Mistakes. Criticism. Gossip. What those five words have in common is that they are some of the nagging problems that face foodservice managers from time to time—and sometimes more often than less. The list can most certainly be extended, but looking at those five problems with managers' eyes and minds can provide a pattern for dealing with other "naggies" that would take a small encyclopedia to catalog. Dealing with changes, stress, mistakes, criticism, and gossip requires some common sense in anticipating management challenges.

Managing Change

Change is required in all phases of our lives if we are to keep pace with a rapidly changing society. Managers must manage change with a flexible, inquisitive attitude and continue to make program improvements for our young people. Truly competent managers do not feel "put upon" when changes are recommended.

"But we have always done it this way," "That won't work," and other clichés signal resistance as managers react to recommended changes. The message is, "I'm happy with the status quo"; "I do not want so-called improvements." Granted that sound tradition must be respected, but managers who refuse to change soon find themselves with programs that have been left behind.

Progress comes from keeping programs updated with current management techniques and tuned to customers' food habits and taste preferences. This is effective change. Managers who succeed make changes when changes are needed or justified. They look at each task or situation and evaluate it. "Is there a better way?" They seek recommendations for improvements and assess them objectively.

Ask some questions *before* you make any change, and then take some deliberate steps to give those changes the best odds for succeeding.

- Is the change necessary? If yes, why? (Be objective in answering this question.)
- Will the change improve the foodservice program for the children?
- Will the change be as good as or better than the old procedure?
- Is this the best time to make the change?

To make effective changes, there are seven steps to follow.

1. Have a clear mental picture of why the changes are needed, what the changes will do for the program and/or the employees, and what results you expect.
2. Explain to the employees the reasons why changes are needed.
3. Avoid the "shock treatment" in announcing changes. If you cannot talk directly with employees affected by the changes, tell them that the changes are coming and hold off making them until they are informed fully.

Did you ever notice that the one assistant you rely on the most complains the least?

4. Discuss the pros and cons of the changes openly with employees, but stress the benefits of the changes.

5. Allow employees to be involved in determining how the changes will take place. Plan cooperatively. List all of the alternatives and select the best one.

6. Observe employee reaction and watch for trouble spots for a few days (or weeks) after the changes are made.

7. Evaluate the changes *as soon as feasible*. And make sure that your evaluation is *objective*.

Managing Stress

Stress is not something confined to a job. Nearly everyone is faced with handling the stresses of family problems and money worries, as well as jobs. A day without pressure or stress can be described as a day without purpose or opportunities, a day with little or no accomplishment. A small amount of pressure or stress can stimulate zealous managers to meet the challenges and to manage their programs more effectively. However, too much *unmanaged* pressure or stress can destroy people and programs. Managers become anxious, irritable, and depressed; blood pressures rise and sleepless nights follow.

Successful managers can make stress work for them. Managing stress is like eating an elephant—you do it one bite at a time. Below are seventeen suggested steps to help you manage stress.

1. Identify the source or reason for the pressure or stress and begin to work out the problems. If you are feeling pressure or tension because there is a problem or misunderstanding between you and an employee, sit down with the employee and talk openly about the differences of opinion. If there is a problem between two employees, you, as a manager, should sit down with both of them and talk openly about the problem until it is resolved or there is a mutual understanding. If unfinished reports or other tasks cause you anxiety and frustration, organize your work day to complete the reports or the jobs first, or at a specific time when there will be a minimum number of interruptions.

2. Pace yourself and your workload. Set your goals and timetables and stick with them. Establish a priority list of "have to," "ought to," and "want to" tasks and complete them one at a time in the order of importance. Make exceptions *only* for emergencies.

3. Manage your time, your most valuable resource. Divide your day into blocks of time and plan activities to fit each block of time. Allow a quiet time for planning and preparing reports, a time for supervising and instructing staff, and so forth.

4. Break down each job into small components. Even the biggest and hardest job becomes easier as each phase of it is completed. Big jobs overwhelm, but small jobs provide self-satisfaction when completed.

5. Take a break when your mind begins to wander and your thinking is no longer sharp and productive.

6. Avoid monotonous routines when possible. Vary the jobs. Keep the work interesting and your productivity keen.

7. Recognize your limits. You cannot be all things to all people and do everything yourself. Learn to delegate so you can keep your workload under control. It is far better to do the most important management functions well and to delegate the less important ones than it is to try to do everything in a haphazard way or to leave work unfinished. Unfinished work is a major source of stress.

8. Establish acceptable standards for yourself and your assistants. Do not expect perfection and put excessive pressure on yourself and others. Relax. Let employees do their jobs, as long as they are performing within acceptable standards. They will produce more and be absent less often.

9. Accept the fact that there are two (or more) sides to any problem. One-sided opinions produce stress. Keep an open mind and look for the other side(s) of the story.

10. Ask for help in solving problems. It releases pressure, helps you see the problem from a different perspective, and lessens your emotional involvement. Asking for help indicates that you have control of the problem. It does not indicate a weakness. Be careful, however, about airing problems with your school friends, neighbors, and outsiders.

11. Adjust your attitude. Look for the positive. There is some good in every situation. Find it. Do not concentrate on failure. Look beyond yourself and your emotions. When you are genuinely interested in helping others, negative-itis flees. Negative-itis produces stress; positive thinking produces healthy attitudes and a good work environment.

12. Keep control of yourself and your emotions. Controlled anger is normal and acceptable. When your anger is kindled or you are in a heated argument, pause a minute and be quiet. Then ask yourself, "Is this issue really worth the anger and frustration?" If it is not, yield to the other person. It will show the other person that you have priorities and that you are in control of yourself and your emotions. Remember that you can win a battle and still lose the war. Getting your way just because it *is* your way is no guarantee of success.

13. Control changes. Look for trends and seek improved methods. Anticipate and predict changes; be prepared; be flexible. Rigid intolerance of changes produces stress.

14. Accept the inevitable. Do not waste time trying to change things that cannot be changed. Trying to change the inevitable raises frustration levels and decreases productivity.

15. Be good to your body. Eat a well-balanced diet and get plenty of rest. When your body is overstretched, stress points are low, frustration levels are high, things appear worse than they really are, and it will be difficult for you to cope with the opportunities that arise. Release tension with exercise. Plan it into your daily schedule, but be sure it is something you enjoy and something that will free your mind from the routine. Exercise can be as strenuous as *you* want it to be.

16. Have fun. Plan to do something you like to do on a regular basis. A hobby, socializing, or whatever you enjoy can release the tension and stress left over from the day's activities. Laughter is a good, healthy emotional outlet.

Did you ever notice that when a child slips you a smile, the next six kids in line look a lot happier?

17. Take time for yourself. Find a quiet time when you can be alone, a quiet place where you can stare into space, clear your mind, and relax. Force yourself to tense and relax your muscles, breathe deeply, and think about pleasant scenes. For a few minutes, make a little world of your own filled with the pleasant things you enjoy, and get away from everything else. Concentrate. After your few quiet minutes, you should be ready to approach the challenges and opportunities of the day with new enthusiasm.

Every person has a unique set of experiences and situations that cause frustration and stress, as well as a personalized way of releasing pressure and managing stress. Find *your* way. It is not only your career but your way of life that depends on it. Make stress work *for* you!

Managing Mistakes

American educator John Erskine wrote that "When you deny people the possibility of making a mistake, you may also be preventing them from developing initiative." That is just another way of saying that every time you take a chance in order to accomplish an important task, you run the risk of making a mistake, but you may also be creating a valuable learning opportunity.

Every one of us makes mistakes. But it is the way we react to mistakes that makes the difference. Good managers regard mistakes as opportunities to develop and grow; poor managers regard mistakes as disasters or disgraces.

The suggestions below can help managers to direct their actions and reactions and to turn their mistakes or the mistakes of their assistants into productive learning opportunities. The unforgivable mistakes are the ones we never learn from.

- Deal with the mistake as quickly as possible.
- Assess the importance of the mistake and look at it in its proper perspective.
- Investigate each mistake to find the cause. *Do not jump to conclusions.*

- Evaluate carefully all explanations and alibis.
- Treat all mistakes objectively, unemotionally, and impersonally.
- Do not show resentment against individuals who make mistakes.
- Take steps to prevent the same mistake from happening again.
- Admit openly and honestly any mistakes that are made.
- Keep criticism constructive, and designed to correct and improve.
- Do not belittle employees and attempt to place blame.
- Keep a record of mistakes and remedies as both a history and a guide for the future.
- Conduct periodic mistake analyses to pinpoint chronic mistake-makers and to determine whether or not employees are assigned to the right jobs.
- Discuss mistakes with employees in private on a personal basis. Do not embarrass assistants in front of others.
- Ask the employee who made the mistake for suggestions to prevent its happening again.
- Initiate controls and follow up to prevent mistakes from occurring again.

Managing Criticism

Criticism is a personal judgment or evaluation. It can be the constructive kind that strengthens people and programs or it can be the destructive kind that ruins people and programs. The difference between constructive and destructive criticism can be the motive and the tone

> *Did you ever notice that some Monday mornings around ten o'clock, you wonder if you really had the weekend off?*

of voice of the person delivering the criticism or the attitude of the person receiving it.

Destructive criticism demoralizes or ridicules. People who use destructive criticism usually do it frequently and rarely offer a solution or suggestions. Such individuals usually are frustrated in their own lives and think that "misery loves company" when someone else makes a mistake. The best way to deal with destructive criticism is to ignore the barbs as much as possible. Do not argue with the person—that is like throwing gasoline on a fire.

Good managers accept constructive criticism gracefully. They accept criticism from another person in the same way that they would want the other person to accept it from them.

Below are some suggestions for managing criticism.

- Listen to the criticism carefully and concentrate on being helpful. People appreciate the person who understands their criticism or complaints.
- Do not take the criticism personally. That is easy to say and sometimes hard to do, but it will be worth the effort.
- Do not make excuses and do not get defensive.
- Thank people for their comments or suggestions and tell them you appreciate their interest in the program. If there is a complaint, ask for specific suggestions to improve the situation. Promise them that you will consider their suggestions.
- Take some time to "let the criticism rest" and to allow you time to think.
- Evaluate the criticism. If changes are needed, make them, and tell the person that the changes have been made. Thank the person for helping you. You will be amazed at the positive reputation that you will build for yourself and your program.
- If you find that the comments are incorrect or the suggestions are impractical, explain to the person why you do not agree. *Do not ignore criticism.* If people take time to make comments or recommendations, they deserve a response, and one that is as objective as possible.

Good managers develop the art of constructive criticism. They criticize the performance of the person and not the person. It is not the words managers use to criticize; it is their attitude when they use the words. Do not put the other person on the defensive. Do not criticize one employee's performance in front of another employee. And do not criticize unless you have an idea for improvement.

When criticism is necessary, the manager should set the stage by "working in" some of the good things the employee has done and then focus on the weak spot that needs improving. Employees have a natural need to feel wanted and to know that their efforts are appreciated.

Constructive criticism can be made to appear as a form of information seeking. For example, you could ask, "How many students do you think will eat the meat loaf made with this recipe?" Be careful with your tone of voice and the way you emphasize the words in this type of criticism. It can spark defensive and negative answers.

Sometimes criticism is a low-key question that indicates that the person is honestly seeking clarification or understanding. The employee might ask, for example: "Please show me again how to cut this cake" or "Please help me get a better understanding of this."

Criticism also may appear as a statement of fact. For example: "These rolls didn't rise today."

Be careful with self-criticism. It will waste time and drain your energy. Instead of holding "pity parties" to feel sorry for yourself as you name your faults one by one, ask yourself, "What can I do now that will help the most?" Answer that question and get busy. Busy, productive people have little time to bask in self-criticism. They separate problems into simple parts and solve them one at a time.

Criticism can be a constructive way to improve people and programs if it is handled properly. Competent managers are responsible for handling criticism professionally.

Managing Gossip

Gossip. The rumor mill. The grapevine. Whatever it is called, this kind of communication travels instantly and destroys people and programs. It grows and changes each time it is repeated. What people hear depends on their background, their priorities, and the mental pictures that they develop while other people are talking. What they think they are saying may not be what others are hearing.

Good, effective communication among the manager and the staff is essential if a program is to continue to grow and improve and if the staff is to continue to enjoy working together to serve young people. If communication between the manager and even one employee becomes strained, you can easily lose the loyalty and cooperation of the others, and frustration will rule.

Every important decision about policy, procedures, and personnel should be announced to all employees at one time. Each employee should have the opportunity to hear the same words said in the same tone and emphasized in the same way. Then ask for questions and answer them to be sure that everyone understands what you have said.

When a person feels compelled to share gossip, it says more about the "gossiper" than the "gossipees." Managers set the stage and provide the role model. They must not gossip to employees or about employees. The manager is responsible for keeping communications in the kitchen open and wholesome.

When gossip rears its ugly head, try asking these "sure-cure" questions.

- Are you *sure* that's correct?
- How do you know?
- What *good* do you expect to come out of this story?
- Who will benefit from that statement?
- Why do you want to repeat it?

If you mince words when it comes to gossip, you run a great risk of mincing your entire operation. Evaluate your own gossip potential with the test that follows. If you find yourself answering yes to any of the questions, begin right now to change your ways. The only thing you have to lose by gossiping is your credibility—and, as a manager, you can *never* afford to lose that.

Gossip Test

	Yes	No
1. Do I spread rumors about other people?		
2. Do I always have good things to say about others?		
3. Do I like to hear reports of a scandal?		
4. Do I judge others only on the basis of facts?		
5. Do I encourage others to bring their rumors to me?		
6. Do I precede my conversations with, "Don't tell anybody . . ."?		
7. Do I keep confidential information confidential?		
8. Do I feel guilty about what I say concerning other people?		
9. Do I accept people at face value?		
10. Do I evaluate people on first impressions?		

(SOURCE: *The Magic of Thinking Big*, by David Schwartz. Prentice-Hall, 1965.)

Did you ever notice that some assistants seem to have more crises in their lives than J. R. Ewing?

The Last Day

A ray of late-afternoon sun fell on Jessie's folded hands as she stared across the kitchen that had been her workplace for thirty years.

The retirement celebrations were over. And what celebrations they had been! Like the one with her "girls," more than forty of them who had worked in her kitchen over the years. Such memories that party generated. . . .

The freshman boy who had had a crush on Mary Lou and finally got up enough courage to invite her to the Halloween Dance. Edie showing up during one National School Lunch Week in a grass skirt that kept molting all over the pineapple. Ginger being crowned Prune Queen when she tried to make chocolate-chip prune cookies and didn't fool one student. The silence that fell over the kitchen for so many days after they buried Edie. A lot of laughter—and some tears.

Then that surprise retirement reception for her in the dining room when she thought she was coming back to school for a PTA meeting. So many people said so many nice things about her and to her. She had no idea why that many people would give up a perfectly good evening to drink punch and eat cookies and talk about her. Three generations of "her" kids. *Dear Lord, I'm old!* Jessie thought. *Three generations!*

But that thought was quickly replaced by memories of faces from that evening. Mayor Jennings announcing that the next day the whole town would celebrate Miss Jessie Day. Her sister, Hester, was there of course. And her brother Jamie and two of his three children from Nashville. Her own kids and beautiful grandchildren. If only Tom had lived....

None of that, Jessie! she thought quickly.

There was old Bill Jenkins.... *Old?* she chuckled to herself. *I'm nearly his age.* And her other "kids." People told her that more than 300 of them had come from as far as Louisville and Atlanta just to be there for "her" day. *Why in heaven's name would they do that for someone who cooked for them at school? But I'm grateful....*

Why am I sitting here? she wondered. *How many days did I dream of when I would be able to call my time my own? How many times had I had to be here when I'd wanted to be somewhere else?* But still she sat. The sun was lower now.

What do I leave here after all these years? What do I leave that will make any difference next September? Nothing much, Jessie thought. But then she reflected: a participation at over 85 percent, money in the bank, Ginger as manager. She would make a good one. She had learned a lot. There was a good staff—positive, competent, flexible, dependable. They helped develop the merchandising program. That would stay and grow and get stronger. And so would the efficiency ratings done for themselves and for the team.

What do I leave here? she wondered again. *Nothing very tangible, but perhaps an attitude, a remembered belief in a program and the purpose for its existence—kids. I hope there's that at least,* Jessie thought.

Jessie suddenly remembered something that she had seen on television years before. It was a history of the Old West. Gary Cooper had narrated it just before he died. Toward the end of the program, he had talked with an old cowboy. Cooper had asked the old man, as he looked back over his life, what he'd change if he could. The old man had thought about the question and then, almost wistfully, had said, "I just wish that we could tear it all down and start over again."

She smiled to herself. *Is that why I'm sitting here on a beautiful May afternoon? Wishing we could tear it down and start all over again? Perhaps,* she thought.

But no, even if that were possible, I wouldn't want that. Too many people. That was it! People. I couldn't have accomplished anything here without those women who have made this kitchen work. Or without those principals who, to varying degrees (boy, did they vary!), put up with my pushiness and lent me a hand when I needed it. And all those kids. They're what it's all about.

No, for better or worse, I did the best I could. But it's other people who make things happen. All any of us can do as individuals is to be ourselves and to try to set the kind of example that causes other people to know that we really care about our profession and what it can do to make someone's life a little better. And to wish always that we could have done more.

And I could have done more, Jessie thought. *I could have given new ideas a better hearing. I could have recognized much earlier the importance of merchandising this program to customers. I could have seen that the efficient use of my assistants' time—their labor—is the key to a successful program's nutritional needs. I could have met that fast-food competition sooner. (Lord knows, our food is better!) I could have realized earlier the value that the computer has as one of our most vital management tools.*

Jessie chuckled to herself. *You could have been president of the United States too, you old fool.*

The foundations for those "could haves" were laid. It would be up to Ginger now. She was the manager. She would be the future.

Jessie stood, turned, and looked out the window and across the school parking lot to the Simpson farm. Cattle grazed sleepily in the late-afternoon sun. Jessie walked to the door and opened it. She glanced back once, and that was all. *That* door closed behind her. Her head was down, and she was deep in thought as she headed toward her car. Halfway there, she was shaken from her reverie by a voice and running feet.

"Miss Jessie! Miss Jessie!" called one and then another. And another.

Jessie turned into the sun and quickly shaded her eyes. Half a dozen young boys—one cradling a basketball—came running toward her. Out of breath, the first to reach her gasped his pleasure in a rush of words. "Miss Jessie, you're still here! Everybody else is gone. We were just shooting baskets and...." The others caught up and clustered around her, all trying to get her attention as they competed to finish one another's words. But she heard what she needed to hear. At that moment.

"We didn't get to say..."

"Goodbye or..."

"Anything."

"It was all for the grownups..."

"And us kids wanted to tell you..."

And then there was silence as heads dropped and sidelong glances were exchanged. Jessie almost chuckled aloud watching six tongue-tied ten-year-olds trying to finish what they had started. And they couldn't.

She reached out and tousled the hair of one of the bent heads. "And I'll miss you, too. Very much." Her voice was husky as she repeated, "Very much."

A moment passed. Nothing was said. Nothing needed to be said.

"Goodbye, boys. And thank you. Thank you." Jessie turned toward her car, which looked distorted by the tears that were close to the surface.

They waved as she pulled away and she waved back. *Thank you, God,* she thought as she turned onto Melrose. *Doors never close. Careers don't end. As long as there is memory and someone remembers. I wonder if Ginger could use some volunteer help next winter—help with those chocolate-chip cookies that those boys like so much.*

Ginger could—and did.

Index

American School Foodservice Association, 22

business sense, 37–38

cafeteria design/decoration, 20
change, management of, 112–14
chemicals, 100–01
cleanliness, 30–31
   schedules for, 82–85
commodities, open-draw, 98–99
   as "something extra," 29–30
common sense, 37
community
   promoting school foodservice to, 22, 25
   student involvement with, 21
computers
   benefits of, 102, 103
   deciding to buy, 102–3
   disadvantages of, 103–4
   fear of, 101–2
   selecting, 104–5
conforming (C) persons, 42, 45–46

contests, 30
criticism, 118–20
customers (students)
   and cafeteria decoration, 20
   and community foodservice, 21
   gauging reactions of, 31–32, 97–98
   involving, in foodservice program, 17–21
   and menu planning, 19–20, 28–29, 97–98
   and nutrition, 20–21
   on Nutrition Advisory Council, 18–19
   and staff attitude, 10, 32
   treatment of, 10, 12–13, 32

decision making, 48–52
delegating, 61, 62
DISC analysis, 42–46
dishroom, 81–82
driving (D) persons, 42, 43–44

Erskine, John, 117

facilities, cleanliness of, 30–31, 82–85
finances, 79, 80
Firm, Connie, 41
food. *See also* Menus; Nutrition; Purchasing
　appearance of, 25, 96
　inventory of, 99
　serving quantity of, 25–26
　waste of, 26, 31, 97
4-Factor Behavioral Model. *See* DISC analysis

garnishes, 25
gossip, 120–22
grooming, 13–15, 32

image
　and attitude, 10, 32
　and cleanliness, 30–31
　and community, 22
　evaluating, 31–32
　factors that determine, 9
　and food appearance, 25
　and food quantity, 25–26
　and menus, 26–30, 32
　and skill, 15
　and speed, 15–16
　and staff appearance, 13–15
　and treatment of customers, 10, 12–13, 17–21, 32
income/expense comparison, 79, 80
Integrative Psychology (Marston), 42
interpersonal (I) persons, 42, 44

job analysis, 71–73

labor. *See* staff

managers
　competency of, 88
　and decision making, 48–52
　positive/negative traits of, 46–48

productivity of, 40–42
qualifications of, 23
qualities of professional, 38–40, 41, 52
and self-criticism, 120
self-inventory by, 42–46
Marston, William M., 42
menus
　acceptability of, to customers, 94–95
　cost of, 95–96
　descriptive terms in, 26–28
　diversity in, 32
　evaluating, 96–97
　importance of, 94
　involving customers in planning, 19–20, 28–29, 97–98
　as marketing tool, 28–30
　nutritional value of, 95, 98
　publishing, 28
　responsibility for planning, 24
　"something extra" on, 29–30, 32
　special-feature, 28–29
　tied in with contests, 30
mistakes, 117–18

National School Lunch Week, 22
negative-itus, 10, 11
nutrition
　involving students in, 20–21, 25
　and menus, 95, 98
Nutrition Advisory Councils, 18–19

¼, ½, ¾ checkpoint system, 95–96

planning, 59–62
production schedules, 75–79
professional, defined, 37
publicity, 22
purchasing, 99–101

reduced-price lunches, 24

schedules
  for cleanup, 82–85
  for dishroom, 81–82
  importance of, 73–75
  of labor requirements, 86–88
  for production, 75–79
  for serving line, 79–81
School Foodservice Program, 22–24
serving line
  appropriate behavior for, 16–17
  attitude of staff on, 10, 79
  importance of efficiency on, 15–16, 80
  scheduling, 79–81
  selecting staff for, 16–17
"something extra," 29–30, 32, 100
stable (S) persons, 42, 45
staff. *See also* Serving line
  appearance of, 13–15, 32
  asking assistance from, 51–52
  attitude of, 10
  communication with, 120–21
  correcting mistakes of, 117–18
  criticizing, 119–20
  delegating responsibilities to, 61, 62
  evaluating, 38
  formulas for scheduling, 86–88
  and gossip, 121
  importance of schedules for, 73–75
  inventory of, 40, 42–46
  job analyses of, 71–73
  preparing, for change, 113–14
stress, 114–17
students. *See* Customers

Things-To-Do list, 59–60
time management, 58–59. *See also* Job analysis
  causes of problems with, 59
  and delegation, 61, 62
  establishing priorities for, 59–60
  evaluating, 62–64
  and planning, 59–62
  and wasting time, 64–65
time wasters, 64–65

workload distribution. *See* Job analysis; Schedules